Journalism Between Disruption and Resilience

Following recent developments in digital technologies, financial crises, and changes in audience preferences, this book addresses the critical challenges and disruptions facing the profession of journalism: an arguably precarious industry suffering from employment insecurity, individualization, and loss of autonomy.

Drawing on research from the Norwegian and Nordic media landscape, *Journalism Between Disruption and Resilience* elaborates on how boundary struggles between journalism and other forms of content, such as marketing and public relations, have become blurred, while social distinctions within the profession are deepened and exacerbated by downsizing and cutbacks in newsrooms and their journalistic staffs. The impact of these developments on the institutional and democratic role of journalism in society is discussed alongside the tensions between professional autonomy and precarious work. Expanding upon several earlier research studies, grounded in the sociology of professions and freelance work, this book provides a new theoretical framework from which to address journalistic precarity and the role of journalism in society.

This is an insightful study for advanced students and researchers in the areas of professional journalism, journalism education, and media industries including marketing and public relations.

Birgit Røe Mathisen is Professor at the School of Journalism, Nord University, Bodø, Norway. Her research interests lie primarily within the profession of journalism, local journalism, media, and democracy. Before entering academic work, she worked as a journalist for 20 years.

Disruptions: Studies in Digital Journalism
Series editor: Bob Franklin

Disruptions refers to the radical changes provoked by the affordances of digital technologies that occur at a pace and on a scale that disrupts settled understandings and traditional ways of creating value, interacting and communicating both socially and professionally. The consequences for digital journalism involve far reaching changes to business models, professional practices, roles, ethics, products and even challenges to the accepted definitions and understandings of journalism. For Digital Journalism Studies, the field of academic inquiry which explores and examines digital journalism, disruption results in paradigmatic and tectonic shifts in scholarly concerns. It prompts reconsideration of research methods, theoretical analyses and responses (oppositional and consensual) to such changes, which have been described as being akin to 'a moment of mind-blowing uncertainty'.

Routledge's book series, *Disruptions: Studies in Digital Journalism*, seeks to capture, examine and analyse these moments of exciting and explosive professional and scholarly innovation which characterize developments in the day-to-day practice of journalism in an age of digital media, and which are articulated in the newly emerging academic discipline of Digital Journalism Studies.

Titles include:

Digital Journalism in China
Edited by Shixin Ivy Zhang

Journalism Between Disruption and Resilience
Reflections on the Norwegian Experience
Birgit Røe Mathisen

Digital-Native News and the Remaking of Latin American Mainstream and Alternative Journalism
Summer Harlow

For more information about this series, please visit: www.routledge.com/ Disruptions/book-series/DISRUPTDIGJOUR

Journalism Between Disruption and Resilience

Reflections on the Norwegian Experience

Birgit Røe Mathisen

LONDON AND NEW YORK

First published 2023
by Routledge
4 Park Square, Milton Park, Abingdon, Oxon OX14 4RN

and by Routledge
605 Third Avenue, New York, NY 10158

Routledge is an imprint of the Taylor & Francis Group, an informa business

British Library Cataloguing-in-Publication Data
A catalogue record for this book is available from the British Library

Library of Congress Cataloging-in-Publication Data
Names: Mathisen, Birgit Røe, author.
Title: Journalism between disruption and resilience: reflections on the
Norwegian experience / Birgit Røe Mathisen.
Description: Abingdon, Oxon; New York, NY: Routledge, 2023. |
Series: Disruptions | Includes bibliographical references and index.
Identifiers: LCCN 2022020837 (print) | LCCN 2022020838 (ebook) |
Subjects: LCSH: Journalism–Social aspects–Norway.
Classification: LCC PN5294 .M38 2023 (print) | LCC PN5294 (ebook) |
DDC 078.481–dc23/eng/20220517
LC record available at https://lccn.loc.gov/2022020837
LC ebook record available at https://lccn.loc.gov/2022020838

ISBN: 978-0-367-70128-4 (hbk)
ISBN: 978-0-367-70130-7 (pbk)
ISBN: 978-1-003-14472-4 (ebk)

DOI: 10.4324/9781003144724

Typeset in Times New Roman
by Deanta Global Publishing Services, Chennai, India

Contents

Illustrations

Figures

Tables

Acknowledgements

As the writing comes to an end, there are many people deserving thanks and acknowledgements for their help and support. First of all, Bob Franklin encouraged me to go ahead with this project and has been a helpful and motivating discussant throughout the process. Also thanks to Priscille Biehlmann and Elizabeth Cox at Routledge for their help and patience.

Thanks to my fellow authors, Lisbeth Morlandstø, Anders Graver Knudsen, Paul Bjerke, and Birgitte Kjos Fonn, for the inspiring and interesting co-writing and discussions. I really enjoyed working with you! The manuscript has also benefitted from comments, critiques, and suggestions from a range of readers, including my colleagues in our research group at Nord University. Special thanks to Lisbeth Morlandstø and Karianne Sørgård Olsen for their extensive reading in the final phase. Thanks to Margareta Salonen for her constructive comments at the Nordmedia conference, where some parts were presented. Thanks to Malene Paulsen Lie for controlling the manuscript and all its references.

And finally and most of all: many thanks to all the journalists who have spent their busy work hours participating in the range of studies that this book builds upon, both through qualitative interview conversations and quantitative surveys. The book couldn't have been written without you. Thank you for bringing essential contributions to our knowledge about journalism and where it is heading!

Bodø
Birgit Røe Mathisen

Authors

Birgit Røe Mathisen is Professor at The School of Journalism, Nord University, Bodø, Norway. Her research interests lie primarily within the profession of journalism, local journalism, media, and democracy. Before entering academic work, she worked as a journalist for 20 years.

Paul Bjerke is Professor at the Faculty of Media and Journalism, Volda University College, Norway. His research interests are media professions and media ecology. Before starting an academic career, Bjerke worked in the media industry for 15 years.

Birgitte Kjos Fonn is Professor of Journalism and Media Studies at Oslo Metropolitan University, Norway. Her main research interests are in media history, political and economic journalism, and the profession of journalism. Fonn worked as a journalist for many years before entering academia.

Lisbeth Morlandstø is Professor at the School of Journalism, Nord University, Bodø, Norway. Her research interests lie primarily within local journalism, media and democracy, and media representation.

Anders Graver Knudsen is senior lecturer at Department of Journalism and Media Studies, Oslo Metropolitan University, Norway. His previous research areas include pedagogic and education, diversity and sports. His background is from photojournalism, working for 10 years in a variety of newspapers, magazines and news agencies.

1 Journalism: between destruction and resilience

Birgit Røe Mathisen

Introduction

Changes in the media landscape and journalistic professional work have led to new understandings and discussions about where to draw the borders of journalism; such boundary disputes are apparent in several countries. In the autumn of 2020 and winter of 2021 a substantive dispute about union membership emerged among Norwegian journalists. A committee within the Norwegian Union of Journalists offered two proposals: (1) to change the union's name to the Media Association, thereby removing the word *journalists*, and (2) to extend the rules of membership, to include those who work with content marketing. The proposal was raised because of changing frameworks and technological developments, which impact on how newsroom work is conducted. As the Chair of the committee stated, 'The members of the union represent far more diversity and complexity than before. Both in name and statutes, the union has to reflect this width'.[1] The proposal generated debate and protest, as well as support. Opponents argue for the necessity to protect the boundaries between free journalism and paid content, and to protect journalistic integrity. 'There is a fundamental barrier between free journalism and paid content. Free journalism is not for sale',[2] stated one in a column. One member even organized a protest campaign, collecting signatures against the proposal, while another claimed, 'Not only shall we sell out our soul, obviously we shall also sacrifice our backbone'.[3] Supporters, however, emphasize that the Norwegian Union of Journalists has increasingly become a union where technologists, directors, producers, researchers, photographers, and so on today feel alienated and believe that a more inclusive union would strengthen the working conditions for all media workers.[4]

Both the proposal itself and the subsequent debate exemplify how disruptions and changes within journalism and media work propagate these constant boundary disputes. In addition, professional identity and

DOI: 10.4324/9781003144724-1

union policy are at stake, which also provoke a debate about who we define as journalists. On the one hand, there is a struggle to protect the 'pure' professional identity, values, and integrity and, on the other, a struggle to reinforce and secure union power, size, and impact. It is certainly not the first struggle of this kind; in fact, the union has engaged in several of them throughout its history. However, although former boundary disputes have been about excluding and narrowing the borders, the new discussion concerns the opposite: to loosen professional borders because of fundamental changes in both the external framework of journalism and professional work.

Journalism as a profession is in a state of flux, experiencing challenges that impact both journalistic professional work and the institution of journalism itself (Peters and Broersma, 2013, 2017; Eide et al., 2016; Lee-Wright et al., 2012). The role of journalism as a democratic infrastructure and profession has been challenged. The institution of journalism shapes the working life of its professionals, and in the middle of these disruptions, journalists are conducting their daily work behind cameras and microphones in traditional newsrooms, in new start-ups, or as individual freelancers, news reporters, digital storytellers, or columnists. The identity of journalism has been existentially shaken, and journalistic ideals have become more ambivalent and liquid. This makes it more relevant than ever to study the professional roles and circumstances of journalists (Hanitzsch, 2018). This book addresses and articulates some of the challenges, disruptions, and boundary disputes confronting the profession of journalism, using the Norwegian experience as a starting point and sources of empirical data. I focus on *journalists* as professionals and an occupational group rather than *the media business*. The aim is to discuss how journalism as a profession is changing and how this impacts upon the institutional role of journalism. As such, the debate among Norwegian journalists about their professional future and destiny, referenced above, could serve as an illustrative introduction to the central issues in this volume. I will return to this specific debate later in the book.

Scholars have frequently asked whether and how journalism might survive as a profession. In a substantial number of scholarly contributions discussing the future of journalism, disruption is acknowledged as a vital concept reflecting a tension between destruction and hope, refracturing and resilience (Peters and Broersma, 2013), disruption and adaption (Eldridge and Broersma, 2018), and crisis and innovation (Ottosen, 2015). However, most of the above literature derives from the Anglo American context. In this chapter, I address the disruption of journalism within a Nordic and Norwegian context, using the 'media welfare state' and the 'Nordic work-life model' as essential frameworks. My aim is to elaborate on three specific tensions within the profession of journalism: 1) pressures between precarity and autonomy, 2) internal shifts in the professional landscape, and 3) boundary disputes. I will also provide an argument setting out why the context of Norway and Scandinavia is of special scholarly interest, describing their particular characteristics regarding both media structures and professional working life. I then focus on the above-mentioned tension between disruption and resilience, elaborate on the discourse about disruption and change within journalism, and outline more thoroughly the three specific identified tensions. Finally, I outline the content and structure of the book.

The Norwegian and Nordic context

The Anglo American imaginary has occupied a central position in scholarly work about journalism (Zelizer, 2015, p. 895). However, crisis has various drivers in different locations, as the external framework, and political and economic forces potentially diverge across contexts. Thus, knowledge about journalism beyond the Anglo American context is an important contribution to the field. This volume discusses disruptions and challenges within the Norwegian media as a starting point.

Norway is a rather small country known for its fjords and mountains, privileged for its salmon and oil income and rendered exotic because of the northern lights and midnight sun. Why would the development of media professionals in this rather sparsely populated country, with an obscure language hardly understood outside the national borders, be of any interest beyond the national context? What can insights from this rather untypical setting bring to a broader understanding of journalism?

Norway is a part of the Nordic region, the northernmost part of Europe, consisting of Norway, Sweden, Denmark, Iceland, and Finland, which have historically been culturally homogenous (Syvertsen et al., 2014). Norway, Sweden, and Denmark are also referred to as Scandinavia. These three countries are often described and treated as one entity because of similarities in cultural history, language, and political governance, and are considered to be among the world's most developed democracies (Sjøvaag, 2019). Norway is a small, stable, and established welfare democracy (Skogerbø and Karlsen, 2021). A vital common denominator for the Nordic countries is the welfare state, which impacts on how journalistic work is organized, as well as the media system and media policy. I will explain these, starting with a brief characterization of the Nordic approach to work-life balance, as the disruptions and boundary disputes in journalism are closely connected to trends in general working life and are affecting journalists' working conditions.

According to the Global Happiness Report, the Nordic countries are continuously rated highly, displaying a strong correlation between working conditions and happiness. 'Critical perspectives on the world's best working lives' is the subtitle of a volume discussing work-life challenges in Nordic countries (Hvid and Falkum, 2019). 'In our view, the essence of the Nordic approach is an extensive organization of opposing interests', state Hvid and Falkum (2019, p. 2). A significant aspect of the Nordic approach is that conflict between employers and workers is recognized and institutionalized in a solvable and productive manner, founded by labour market organizations that provide legitimacy and power. The third component in this relationship is the state, which takes a mediating role if the parties cannot reach an agreement. This tripartite agreement is a vital characteristic of the Nordic model; it represents a triangle of employers' associations, trade unions, and the state, which constitute a balance of power and a constructive, if occasionally conflictual, partnership (Hvid et al., 2019, p. 12; Dølvik et al., 2015). Collective organization and negotiated compromise are significant, and the two sides of the labour market recognize each other's existence and eligibility (Hvid et al., 2019, p. 10). The tripartite agreement is strongly connected to relatively large welfare states offering collective solutions regarding childcare, education, elderly care, pensions, and laws regulating work-life balance. The result is highly market-oriented communities that at the same time embrace high levels of solidarity and equality. The working conditions, wages, and employment security are better than in many other countries, and union density is relatively high. Workers in Nordic countries enjoy a high degree of influence on the labour market (Norbäck, 2021, p. 3). Consequently, disruption and change, such as downsizing and loss of jobs, would still leave professionals in Nordic countries with a stronger safety net than in many other countries.

A culture characterized by trust and a high degree of social capital is considered to be a vital explanation for the Nordic model and its history. The model has its origin in conflicts that arose in the late 19th century between employers and employees (Falkum et al., 2019, p. 34), and it was developed and formatted in the social democratic era from 1935. However, neoliberal flows have also impacted on Nordic countries. Globalization has led to more flexible and individualized working conditions, declining union membership, and growing demands for efficiency. Thus, the Nordic model is under pressure (Hvid et al., 2019, pp. 27–28). Crises and changes take place even in the peaceful corners of the world (Skogerbø et al., 2021, p. 15). For journalism and the media business, a significant consequence of change and disruption is the loss of jobs. News media have experienced large-scale downsizing and lay-offs in recent years, prompting a lesser availability of journalistic work. The Norwegian Union of

Journalists lost 1500 members between 2011 and 2019, which has reduced current membership to 8000 (Bjerke et al., 2019, p. 21). New graduates strive to find regular jobs, while experienced journalists lose their jobs (Örnebring, 2009). A distinct characteristic of the disruption of journalism is increased precarity and job insecurity (Deuze and Witschge, 2018); thus, precarity becomes a key characteristic of contemporary journalistic work (Örnebring, 2009, p. 1). According to Kalleberg (2009, p. 2), precarious work is 'employment that is uncertain, unpredictable, and risky from the view of the worker'. As a concept, precarity has been used in several scholarly works about the increasing number of freelancers (Mathisen, 2016; Cohen, 2016; Norbäck, 2021).

These developments are not specific to the media business – however, they are tied to a neoliberalistic turn that contributes to individualization and employment insecurity in general (Beck, 2000; Giddens, 2007). Work-life flexibility is an ongoing and general trend (Sennett, 2008) geared towards individualization and employment insecurity in neo-capitalism, which affects Nordic countries as well, even though the welfare state provides citizens with a relatively solid safety net compared to many other countries. The media industries seemingly provide an early indicator of such changes (Sørensen et al., 2005) and provide some very illustrative case studies of these economically motivated structural changes (Örnebring, 2009). Thus, studying journalists working within the frames of the Nordic model is a vital way to explore consequent disruptions and the boundary disputes that have arisen.

The media welfare state

Hallin and Mancini (2009) classify the relations between media and political systems. They place Norway, along with other Nordic countries, within what they term the 'Democratic Corporatist' model, characterized by an early and strong development of journalistic professionalism, a relatively high level of journalistic autonomy, and an active role for the state. However, the systems that Hallin and Mancini described and classified have already changed fundamentally in relation to the dimensions they used. Still, their typology has thoroughly influenced Nordic research and continues to do so (Skogerbø et al., 2021, p. 20). Being placed between the state and the market, the development of journalism in the Nordic countries is of special scholarly interest (Sjøvaag, 2019). Nordic countries constitute a distinct cultural and geographic entity among the world's nations, and they share the common Nordic model (Syvertsen et al., 2014, p. 4) outlined above. A distinct organization of media and communication has evolved in Nordic countries, with public support, an independent press, high readership, and publicly funded broadcasting serving as vital aspects. Syvertsen et al. (2014) describe this as a 'media welfare state', arguing that the Nordic media systems are sufficiently distinct to stand out in the world. They define the media welfare state as based upon the following four pillars: a cultural media policy, universal services, editorial freedom, and consensual and durable policy solutions, rooted in an understanding of media as a public good. The media policy aims to sustain diversity and quality.

However, the Nordic model is generally described in positive terms, and Sivertsen et al. (p. 7) ask whether it is being glorified and romanticized, glossing over difficult questions and internal tensions. Further, they point out that neoliberalism, globalization, and changing demographics undermine the Nordic model. Similarly, Sjøvaag (2019, p. 33) points to challenges inflicted upon the media welfare state model: public service broadcasting, for example, is under attack from private media operators. Circulations and revenues are declining, and advertising has moved to global actors such as Facebook and Google. However, while discussing challenges to the media welfare state, Syvertsen et al. (2014, p. 123) conclude that continuity is as important as change, with editorial freedom, diversity in content, and cultural policy goals serving as stabilizing factors. Also, the level of trust in the news media and political institutions is high in all Nordic countries (Skogerbø et al., 2021, p. 17). Despite downsizing and revenue loss in Norway, both readership and circulation are still relatively high, as well as the willingness to pay for online news.

When describing the Norwegian media field, the geographical aspect cannot be overlooked, as it is characterized by a stratified geographical pattern with a large amount of local and regional newspapers published widely across the country (Høst, 2005). In addition, the national broadcaster (NRK) has 48 district or local offices distributed through the country, where 900 of the 3400 NRK staff are employed (Mathisen, 2021). Consequently, a substantial number of journalists *are* local or, at the very least, *have been* local for part of their professional lives. A common career path is to start off in small, local newsrooms as newcomers to the profession and then move on to larger newsrooms later.

Within the media welfare state, media and journalism are regarded as public goods, with institutional tasks securing citizenship and civic participation. Journalism as a profession depends upon a legitimacy underlining its institutional role. The disruption of journalism engages not only its professional workers and scholars of journalism studies but also politicians. A committee appointed by the Norwegian government expressed concern that the pressure upon journalism may become so strong that journalists and journalism will no longer be able to fill their roles in the democratic infrastructure:

Due to fundamental, structural changes caused by global competition, technological developments and changed audience behavior, we lack resilient business models to finance essential parts of societally important journalism.

(NOU, 2017: 7, p. 9)

The concern of this volume is about journalism as a profession. Nevertheless, how journalism faces and manages the disruptions and challenges, as well as how society meets and deals with them, has consequences far beyond its professionals and their working conditions, as underlined by the concern expressed above. Representing a democratic infrastructure in the public sphere, the future of journalism also has a vital impact upon civic engagement and public discourse.

Destruction or resilience? A discourse about disruption

Changes, challenges, disruptions, and an uncertain future are a concern for journalism professionals and the media industry, as well as for scholars of journalism studies, politicians, and citizens – for three particular reasons. First, disruptions in *working conditions* refer to job losses, downsizing, and cutbacks, thus resulting in fewer journalists and a shrunken profession, where an increasing number of journalists work under precarious conditions. Second, *technology* is also a concern because technological development affects workflow, user preferences, and audience behaviour, thus bringing fundamental changes to societal communication. Finally, *economy and business models* are also affected, and revenue streams vanish and raise a fundamental question: how is journalism to be financed? These three reasons for concern are aspects of change in the *exterior framework* of journalism, affecting *internal aspects within the profession* – for example, an eroding autonomy and professional authority.

The literature on these disruptions has addressed both challenges, as well as the restructuring of journalism focusing on the tension between doomsday and hope, as mentioned earlier. The first discusses whether there is, consequently, *de-professionalization* when the profession shrinks and economic forces triumph over professional values. The latter highlights resilience and reinforced professional ideals and values, underlining that journalism has always encountered changes, challenges, and disruptions but continues to adapt. New technology has also improved journalism, and multiskilling has empowered professionals. The latter might also be seen as a *re-professionalization* of journalism.

Recently, several books with the prefix '*re*' in the title have been published about journalism – *re-thinking* (Peters and Broersma, 2013,

2017), *re-inventing* (Waisbord, 2013), and *re-examining* (Eide, Sjøvaag, and Larsen, 2016) offer some examples. Further, there are publications using *change* as a vital title word: *Changing journalism* (Lee-Wright et al., 2012), *Journalism in change* (Nygren et al., 2015), and *Journalism and change* (Örnebring, 2018) reflect this trend. In addition, a considerable number of scholarly articles has analyzed the change, challenge, innovation, and disruption of journalism as an institution and as professional work, as well as the consequences of its societal role and democratic infrastructure.

Zelizer (2015) raises critical questions about how the institution of journalism deals with uncertainty; further, she offers a critical discussion on the discursive shape of the term *crisis*. Drawing on Fairclough (1995, cited in Zelizer, 2015, p. 891), she underlines the impact of the discursive convention typically used when addressing complicated institutional contours, stressing that members of an institution drive processes of institutionalization by producing influential texts that change the discourse on which the institution depends (Zelizer, 2015, p. 891). In this way, she points to the fact that a great deal of the discourse on crisis is driven by journalists themselves. Following this, it is of vital interest to explain how both scholars in the field and practitioners talk about and define changes and challenges. Are the changing dynamics in the journalistic field seen as a form of disruption, upsetting familiar ways of doing things, or are they seen as an opportunity for adaption (Eldridge and Broersma, 2018)?

This dichotomy is central in the volume *Rethinking Journalism* from 2013 (Peters and Broersma, 2013). The book argues that the problems of journalism are far more structural than is often voiced and that the profession has to redefine itself fundamentally, especially in relation to trust and participation. In the book, authors discuss the future prospects of journalism through two distinctive and contradictory views: refracture or resilience? Marcel Broersma describes journalism as a profession suffering from osteoporosis – that is, a refractured paradigm:

> Essentially, the crisis of journalism [reflects] the vanishing authority and vaporizing trust because citizens have more access to information and can assess alternative representations of social reality. Currently, journalism is a profession suffering from osteoporosis.
>
> (Broersma, 2013, p. 44)

He states that the crisis of journalism is not just a crisis of technology or an outdated business model; the problem is rather first and foremost that journalism is struggling to survive in a new age by means of a paradigm that suited an era that is quickly becoming history. To survive, he claims, journalism needs to redefine itself (p. 29). In the same volume though, Michael Schudson argues for a more optimistic view of the future. He describes journalism as a resilient profession, as 'birch trees whose trunks in the storms of winter bend very far over without breaking' (Schudson, 2013, p. 195). He underlines that journalism has always faced changes and has managed to adopt and exemplify several large transformation processes from the 1960s: 'None of these developments have been without losses, but the gains have been very large and in the digital transformation, those gains are growing still' (p. 195). Zelizer (2015, p. 897) also illustrates that the changing technological parameters of digital media are not new but repeat performances. She provides an example of the radio/press wars of the 1920s and 1930s and the introduction of television in the 1950s and 1960s in the US. In both cases, questions about what it means to be a journalist and who should deliver the news to the public were proposed (p. 898). Among most journalists, TV reporters were regarded as second-class citizens in television's early days (p. 899). In other words, this functioned as an expression of how some parts of the professional field of journalism could win more prestige than others.

Returning to Schudson and Broersma's discussion about crisis or refracture, resilience or development: the concepts of osteoporosis and solid birch trees are quite divergent associations. Four years later, Peters and Broersma (2017) edited a new volume, entitled *Rethinking Journalism Again – Societal Role and Relevance in the Digital Age*. The editors state in their introduction that 'Technological advancement and economic models are typical culprits identified in terms of how they are disrupting journalism practice and the news, and impacting journalism's ability – both positively and negatively – to deliver on its historical promises'. They proceed with a discussion on how this development challenged the societal role and public relevance of journalism, and they underline that the pace of change in the media ecology has been exceptionally rapid over the past couple of decades, which means that disruption appears to be constant (p. 7).

Eide and Sjøvaag (2016, p. 3) use the term *re-orientation*, to analyze how the institution of journalism responds to profound changes in its social and professional practices, norms and values. Using the term re-orientation, Eide advocates for a distance to the approach of death and collapse (McChesney and Pickard, 2011) and tries to strike a balance between the success and decay paradigms (Eide, 2016, p. 17). Eide argues for an institutional re-orientation and concludes, rather optimistically, that

> Journalism evolves and reorients through processes of interaction – with technology, ownership, audiences, other fields – tradition and change going hand in hand. Journalism is changing, and is to some extent challenged, but is as relevant as ever, perhaps even more so.
>
> (Eide, 2016, p. 224)

Elizabeth Hansen (2020) claims that digital disruptions in journalism are issues of control and transparency in news work. Her discussion reflects the same tension; on the one hand, they are seen as a portending disaster, often connoting a death sentence and provoking fear and anxiety. On the other, they represent a magical remedy, a term of choice that has helped a variety of established actors to navigate a crisis of considerable uncertainty and complexity. Thus, disruption provides a powerful vocabulary of motivation and justification for change. According to Hansen (2020, p. 177), the use of digital disruption as a term to describe changes in the field of journalism has led to an increased focus on the disruption of business models and the collapse of the newsroom. However, she argues that it is the deeper disruptions in the values and practices of journalism which have brought the field to a point of existential crisis. In other words, her perception focuses on the profession of journalism and professional work rather than the media as an industry.

Ryfe (2019) discusses disruption, arguing for a curious resilience of some aspects of traditional journalism within a generally disruptive environment. He applies a practice perspective, underlining that journalism as an occupational field is held together by shared cultural practices. He states that journalism has never been stable or free from the push and pull that defines it as a social field. However, by the mid-20th century, the occupation became the most stable it has ever been (p. 849). Ryfe argues that the autonomy of journalism began to wane in the 1970s as journalism became increasingly commercialized and politicized. When the internet arrived, more people gained the ability to publish news, and the sphere of public communication enlarged. Simultaneously, however, the commercial underpinnings of modern journalism were severely damaged. The consequence was that 'more and different kinds of people and organizations are producing news in the social space once occupied solely by journalists' (Ryfe, 2019, p. 849). This process made it more difficult to make distinctions between journalism and other kinds of content production, he continues. Also, Ryfe highlights the dynamic interaction between new and old actors in the field, simultaneously reproducing longstanding journalistic practices and introducing new ones: in other words, new and old, challenge and change, but still resilience.

Is there a before and after – that is, journalism as it used to be, and journalism as it has become? Zelizer (2015) offers diverging discursive responses: whether we are seeing a crisis as something that is resolvable and that can be overcome or as something that is destructive and apocalyptic (p. 896). She suggests that transformation is always more gradual than a before/after narrative. Zelizer, Schudson (2013), and Ryfe (2019) underline the continuous instability and change in journalism (i.e., constant development and changes) due to an external framework and relationship with other social fields. Lee-Wright, Philips, and Witschge (2012, p. xi) similarly underline the ever-changing status of journalism: 'Journalism has always been in a field of flux, and we do not envisage it will become a homogenous field in the future'. In their volume *Changing journalism*, the authors explore the way in which journalism is changing and discuss the consequences of journalism's democratic role.

Journalism is forever changing and forever becoming, according to Deuze and Witschge (2020, p. 126), when researching journalistic entrepreneurs. They observe how chaos and crisis in media businesses are perceived as an opportunity for journalistic start-ups. The discourse of crisis in journalism is associated with a loss of capacity for news media to effectively form a fourth estate (p. 119). In this context, start-up journalists want to make a difference in order to fulfil a need for society and to bring innovation to those places they consider lacking in the legacy media contest (p. 122). However, Deuze and Witschge also touch on the perception of entrepreneurial journalism:

> Understanding the future of journalism through the lens of entrepreneurial journalism is not neutral or unambiguous – it favours a particular form of journalism, a form we shall question for its precarious basis and the blindness for systemic critique.
>
> (Deuze and Witschge, 2020, p. 109)

'The greatest truism for contemporary journalism studies is "journalism is changing"', writes Henrik Örnebring (2018, p. 555). He points out that, historically, journalism studies have focused on the fact that journalism has not changed; on the contrary, it has been exceptionably stable. However, from the 1970s and the 1980s onwards, technology businesses and the organizations of labour began to change, and journalistic research became increasingly concerned with studying these changes. He argues that professionalization, commercialization, and digitalization are dominant aspects to understand with regards to these changes. However, he argues that changes are under-theorized in the field: there is rich empirical and descriptive research on all aspects of change, he argues, but little theorization on how to explain these changes.

Changes in working conditions

The changes discussed above, in turn, affect journalists' working conditions. Gollmitzer (2020, p. 2) states that the study of employment conditions in journalism scholarship and research has been too long neglected and is only just emerging. Following the same argument, Cohen (2019, p. 572) emphasizes that 'a labour perspective will become increasingly important for journalism researchers as journalism further digitizes, conflict and struggle around the conditions of those who produce journalism intensifies, as the ongoing unionization wave in digital newsroom demonstrates'. Journalism is a profession in decline, where the number of employed journalists shrinks and the number of freelancers grows. Consequently, there is a rise in precarious employment (Gollmitzer, 2020; Bredart and Holderness, 2016; Deuze and Witschge, 2020). Gollmitzer states that the growth in individualized, contingent, and freelance labour leads to a de-institutionalization of labour.

Journalists face an increased volume and pace of work, which prompts multi-tasking and instant-publishing demands inherent to digital technology and managerial control (Cohen, 2019; Lamark and Morlandstø, 2019; Comor and Compton, 2015; Olsen, 2018). Cohen (2019) analyzes the work experiences of digital journalists, professionally engaged in the constant flow of online news production. She identifies three major characteristics shaping their work. First, *measurability* is the drive to produce content that will be widely circulated, read and shared by an audience on social media, and this is where analytics becomes a vital force that could undermine journalistic autonomy and news judgements. Second, *intensification of work* refers to the increased speed of production, multiskilling, and the blurring of the borders between work and non-work time. Third, *commodification* is where circulation and distribution become key elements of journalistic work, and this re-orients journalists towards the market and commercial values.

Ottosen (2015) discusses how the profession of journalism has developed historically from party press to market-driven journalism, which has had a dramatic impact on the working conditions along seven formative cleavage lines. One of them is the struggle to create unions, another is the struggle for intellectual property rights, while yet another is the struggle for freedom of expression. Ottosen's work also reflects the tension between crisis and optimism as described above, raising the question, crisis or innovation? He concludes rather optimistically, underlining the role of a strong union:

> Despite the present challenges, the idea of professional identity and relative autonomy for individual journalistic practice has survived. A strong national trade union for journalists and other social structures based on the cleavages in the area of intellectual property rights, ethics, the boundaries between other occupations and the struggle for education have had an impact upon journalistic room and independence.
>
> (Ottosen, 2015, p. 213)

The social structures he describes are anchored in the Nordic model and the media welfare state: intellectual property rights are secured through agreements within the conflict partnership, and the ethical norms are supported by both sides.

As the discussion in the previous pages shows, scholars and professionals vary in how they talk about the discussion and changes in journalism. The words and concepts used do have an impact on how we perceive, interpret, and understand the development of journalism. Are journalists moving from safety and stability to a new and uncertain future in a state of crisis and uncertainty, which will damage the profession and society, or are we facing a new phase in the eternal and everlasting development of a profession where journalism continually changes and adapts? This book argues the latter. Journalism has always changed along with technology and society. However, development still *changes* journalism and challenges its role, which gives reason to take the concerns expressed by scholars seriously. In parallel, technology changes the entire societal communication, in which journalism is a core practice, underlining the continuous need for scholarly attention to where these changes are leading. Further, we require knowledge about what this implies for the professionals carrying out journalistic work, as well as how journalism plays a societal and democratic role.

Three tensions within the profession

The journalistic field is huge and wide, and my ambition is not to embrace the entire field or its framework. This volume aims to shed light on some selected parts of the profession to a greater extent than others. Throughout the following empirical chapters in this book, I elaborate on three tensions within the profession: first, *pressures between precarity and autonomy*; second, *internal cleavages and rifts within the profession of journalism and shifts within the professional landscape*; and third, *boundary disputes*. The first tension is mainly concerned with professionals' working conditions, the second is related to journalism as a stratified field with internal cleavages between its centre and periphery, while the third focusses on how the profession draws a demarcation line towards its surroundings. As such, the book addresses questions affecting internal aspects of the profession, as well as how the profession relates to its surroundings.

Between precarity and autonomy

Journalism studies has traditionally been characterized by a newsroom centricity (Wahl et al., 2009); however, journalism increasingly takes place outside newsrooms and traditional institutions. Cutbacks and downsizing lead to a shrinking profession and an increasing number of journalists finding themselves in short-term contracts or precarious working conditions: atypical labour, freelancing, and part-time work (Deuze and Witschge, 2018; Mathisen, 2016). We cannot explain journalism simply by looking at established news media companies; journalists can also be seen in freelance agencies, independent start-ups, and so on (Deuze and Witschge, 2020, p. 22–28). Journalists are working under increasing commercial pressures (Gollmitzer, 2020). Some academics have argued that digital technologies improve journalists' working conditions, leading to increased transparency and participation (Meier, 2007), which suggests that multiskilling allows for greater autonomy and creativity, as well as increased time efficiency (Nygren, 2014). Others, however, have suggested that digital technologies trigger deskilling, increased computerization, and the automatization of labour, reducing both craft and creativity and resulting in heavier workloads and more journalists tied to their desks (Lee-Wright et al., 2012; Örnebring, 2010; Cohen, 2019). At the same time, the concept of entrepreneurial journalism showcases a growing creative group of professionals enjoying freedom, autonomy, and control over their own work (Singer, 2017; Deuze and Witschge, 2018).

Building upon the former discussion in this chapter between doomsday and resilience, the tension here is apparent, with some scholars claiming that these trends disrupt the profession, blur professional borders, and limit professional autonomy. Others have counterclaimed that independent freelancers, entrepreneurs, and journalistic start-ups could strengthen professional values and that digital technologies might stimulate transparency and public trust. One could also use the discrepancy between de-professionalization and re-professionalization. The first highlights a consequential damage to professional autonomy, and the latter shows that an emerging and growing amount of independent and autonomous news workers have strengthened their professional values. Journalistic start-ups might be created based on a dissatisfaction with commercialization in traditional news media, and the start-ups might provide high standards of investigative journalism, underlining professional values (Wagemans et al., 2016). What emerges from this is a tension about whether journalism as a profession experiences a de- or re-professionalization, or a deskilling or multiskilling, which will be further investigated in this volume.

Shifting landscape and cleavages within the profession

However, the abovementioned developments also raise concerns about whether this leads to deeper divisions within the profession of journalism. Hierarchies within the newsroom have become destabilized (Ryfe, 2019, p. 849). Inspired by Bourdieu, Hovden (2008, p. 138) analyzes the profession of journalism as a socially stratified field:

In the sector of great journalistic prestige we find the largest newspapers and specialist press, the great editors, the columnist and almost every sign of journalistic capital: editorial control, prizes, juries, control over unions, public notoriety etc.

In the region of lowest journalistic prestige, we find among others, local journalists, freelancers, and young journalists in temporary jobs. Thus, it is clear that some journalists enjoy high prestige, are profiled as star journalists, and achieve prestigious and professionally satisfying jobs as columnists, investigative reporters, and digital storytellers, whereas others are trapped in computerized and automated work, rewriting and linking the work of others (Nygren, 2008). The distinction between the highly qualified, profiled, and prestigious work of some journalists, compared to the routinized, precarious, and computerized work of others, is also reflected in highly differentiated working conditions and job security. Changes in the journalistic framework contribute to the creation of new hierarchies within the professional field of journalism (Wiik, 2015, p. 120). Using Swedish journalism as a starting point, Jenny Wiik discusses whether journalism has remained a cohesive profession or is fracturing into smaller groups and sub-identities. She describes a professional field where some groups gain low status and others high, and where professional autonomy is a privilege reserved for a few highly profiled journalists with specialist skills (Wiik, 2015, p. 131). A vital question is how these cleavages affect the professional ideal of journalism, as well as whether the hierarchy is changing. Functional flexibility relates to the division of the workforce into a multi-skilled core and a large periphery of semi-affiliated professionals. A core segment of journalists is enjoying greater job security and career development, whereas the peripheral group tends to be temporarily employed in subcontracted or project-related arrangements (Deuze and Witschge, 2020, p. 30). However, hierarchy might also change, and internal power could shift (Bjerke et al., 2019).

Boundary disputes

According to Carlson and Lewis (2015, p. 3), 'Journalism is not a solid, stable thing, but a constantly shifting denotation'. Digital media technologies blur the borders of journalism. Boundary work is about the legitimate power to define, describe, and explain (Carlson, 2015). The parallel concept of jurisdiction describes how a profession asks society to recognize its cognitive structure through exclusive rights (Abbott, 1988). Boundary disputes are not a new phenomenon in journalism; they have been a part of its history. The previously mentioned perception of television journalists as second class in the early days of television (Zelizer, 2015, p. 899) stands as one example of boundary disputes as repeat performances. The capacity to endure has remained front and centre in the institutional discourses through which journalism distinguishes itself from other modes of public expression (Zelizer, 2015, p. 896). Vital for discussion is whether the disruption of journalism leads to new forms of boundary disputes and how these are enacted. A crucial boundary dispute to discuss is the one between journalism and public relations (PR) and communication work, as the latter increases and employs a rising number of workers.

The structure of the book

I elaborate further on all three tensions described above throughout the empirical chapters. The book contains six chapters. Following this introduction, Chapter 2 sets out the theoretical groundwork and analytical foundation for the book, discussing how the sociology of professions could better illuminate the current disruption of journalism, as well as how this impacts on the institutional role of journalism. In Chapter 3, co-authored with Paul Bjerke and Birgitte Kjos Fonn, we describe the professional landscape, aiming to analyze internal shifting movements in the professional hierarchy. Chapter 4 is also empirically based, shedding light on the working conditions for freelance journalists and is co-authored with Anders Graver Knudsen. The chapter addresses the double-edged nature of self-employment, focusing on freelancers' issues with precarity and autonomy, as well as boundary disputes. Chapter 5 moves the focus from freelancers to highly profiled columnists (i.e., the important stars and brands for many media companies) and is co-authored with Lisbeth Morlandstø. We discuss the role, professional status, and authority of columnists in the changing media environment, addressing the shifting professional hierarchy. Finally, Chapter 6 concludes and collects the threads from the previous empirically based chapters (i.e., Chapters 3, 4, and 5) to construct an overarching discussion about how the disrupted profession might deal with the future.

Notes

1 www.medier24.no/artikler/vil-endre-navnet-til-norsk-journalistlag-til-medie-forbundet/502480
2 www.medier24.no/artikler/gar-ut-mot-njs-foreslatte-navneendring-vil-stille-sporsmal-ved-var-integritet/502500
3 https://journalisten.no/kortnytt-medieforbundet-nj/ikke-bare-skal-vi-selge-sjelen-vi-skal-apenbart-ogsa-kvitte-oss-med-ryggraden/436207
4 https://journalisten.no/eskil-wie-furunes-kortnytt-medieforbundet/medieforbundet-er-det-beste-forslaget-pa-lenge/436691

References

Abbott, A. (1988) *The System of Professions: an Essay on the Division of Expert Labor*. Chicago: University of Chicago Press.

Beck, U. (2000) *The Brave New World of Work*. Cambridge: Polity Press.

Bjerke, P., Fonn, B.K. and Mathisen, B.R. (eds.) (2019) *Journalistikk, profesjon og endring* Stamsund: Orkana Akademisk. [Journalism, a profession in change].

Bredart, H. and Holderness, M. (2016) *Rights and Jobs in Journalism: Building Stronger Unions in Europe*. Brussels: European Federation of Journalists.

Broersma, M. (2013) A refractured paradigm: Journalism, hoaxes and challenge of trust. In Peters, C. & Broersma, M. (eds). *Rethinking Journalism. Trust and Participation in a Transformed News Landscape*. London: Routledge, pp. 28–45.

Carlson, M. (2015) Introduction: The many boundaries of journalism. In Carlson, M. and Lewis, S. (eds.) *Boundaries of Journalism. Professionalism, Practices and Participation*. London and New York: Routledge, pp. 1–19.

Carlson, M. and Lewis, S. (2015) *Boundaries of Journalism. Professionalism, Practices and Participation*. London and New York: Routledge.

Cohen, N. (2016) *Writers' Rights: Freelance Journalism in a Digital Age*. Montreal & Kingston: McGill-Queen's University Press.

Cohen, N. (2019) At work in the digital newsroom. *Digital Journalism*, 7(5), pp. 571–591. DOI: 10.1080/21670811.2017.1419821

Comor, E. and Compton J. (2015) Journalistic labour and technological fetishism. *The Political Economy of Communication*, 3(2), pp. 74–87.

Deuze, M. and Witschge, T. (2018) Beyond journalism: Theorizing the transformation of journalism. *Journalism*, 19(2), pp. 165–181. DOI: 10.1177/1464884916688550

Deuze, M. and Witsgche T. (2020) *Beyond Journalism*. Cambridge: Polity Press.

Dølvik, J.E., Fløtten, T., Hippe, J.M. and Jordfald, B. (2015) *The Nordic Model Towards 2030. A New Chapter? NordMod2030*. Final report. Oslo: Fafo-Report, 2015:07.

Eide, M. (2016) Journalistic re-orientations. In Eide, M., Sjøvaag, H. and Larsen, L.O. (eds.) *Journalism Re-examined: Digital Challenges and Professional Reorientations. Lessons from Northern Europe*. Bristol, UK and Chicago: Intellect, pp. 15–27.

Eide, M. and Sjøvaag, H. (2016) Journalism as an institution. In Eide, M., Sjøvaag, H. and Larsen, L.O. (eds.) *Journalism Re-examined: Digital Challenges and Professional Reorientations. Lessons from Northern Europe*. Bristol UK and Chicago: Intellect, pp. 1–15.

Eide, M., Sjøvaag, H. and Larsen, L.O. (eds.) (2016) *Journalism Re-examined: Digital Challenges and Professional Reorientations. Lessons from Northern Europe*. Bristol, UK and Chicago: Intellect.

Eldridge, S. and Broersma, M. (2018) Encountering disruption: Adaptation, resistance and change. *The Journal of Applied Journalism and Media Studies*, 7(3), pp. 469–479. DOI: 10.1386/ajms.7.3.469_1

Falkum, E., Hvid, H. and Hansen, P.B. (2019) The peculiar history of Nordic Working life. In Hvid, H. and Falkum E. (eds.) (2019) *Work and Wellbeing in*

the Nordic Countries. Critical Perspectives on the World's Best Working Lives.
London and New York: Routledge, pp. 30–46.

Giddens, A. (2007) *Europe in the Global Age.* Cambridge: Polity Press.

Gollmitzer, M. (2020) Employment conditions in Journalism. *Oxford Research Encyclopedia of Communication,* pp. 1–28. https://doi.org/10.1093/acrefore/9780190228613.013.805

Hallin, D.C., & Mancini, P. (2009) *Comparing Media System: Three Models of Media and Politics.* Cambridge: Cambridge University Press.

Hansen, E. (2020) Disrupting the news. *Sociologica,* 14(2), pp. 1971–8853. https://doi.org/10.6092/issn.1971-8853/11177

Hanitzsch, T. (2018) Roles of journalists. In Vos, T.P. (ed.) *Journalism.* Boston: De Gruyter Inc. DOI: 10.1515/9781501500084

Høst, S. (2005) *Det lokale avismønsteret: dekningsområder, mangfold og konkurranse 1972–2002.* [The local newspaper landscape]. Fredrikstad: Institutt for journalistikk.

Hovden, J.F (2008) *Profane and sacred: a study of the Norwegian journalistic field.* Phd-thesis, University of Bergen.

Hvid, H. and Falkum E. (eds.) (2019) *Work and Wellbeing in the Nordic Countries. Critical Perspectives on the World's Best Working Lives.* London and New York: Routledge.

Hvid, H., Falkum, E. and Steen, A.H. (2019) Nordic working life shaped through conflicts and compromises. In Hvid, H. and Falkum E. (eds.) *Work and Wellbeing in the Nordic Countries. Critical Perspectives on the World's Best Working Lives.* London and New York. Routledge, pp. 9–30.

Kalleberg, A. (2009) Precarious work, insecure workers: Employment relations in transition. *American Sociological Review,* 74, pp. 1–22. DOI: 10.1177/000312240907400101

Lamark, H. and Morlandstø, L. (2019) Snakker journalister fortsatt med folk? In Bjerke, P., Fonn, B.K. and Mathisen, B.R. (eds.) *Journalistikk, profesjon og endring.* Stamsund: Orkana Akademisk. [Journalism, a profession in change].

Lee-Wright, P. Philips, A. and Witschge, T. (2012) *Changing Journalism.* London and New York: Routledge.

Mathisen, B.R. (2016) Entrepreneurs and Idealists: Freelance Journalists at the Intersection of Autonomy and Constraints. *Journalism Practice,* 11(7), pp. 909–924. DOI: 10.1080/17512786.2016.1199284

Mathisen, B.R. (2021) Sourcing practice in local media: Diversity and media shadows. *Journalism Practice,* pp. 1–19. https://doi.org/10.1080/17512786.2021.1942147

McChesney, R. and Pickard, V. (2011) *Will the Last Reporter Please Turn Out the Lights? The Collapse of Journalism and What Can Be Done to Fix It.* New York: The New Press.

Meier, K. (2007) Innovations in Central European newsrooms. *Journalism Practice,*1(1), pp. 4–19. DOI: 10.1080/17512780601078803

Norbäck, M. (2021) Back to the future of journalistic work? *Entrepreneurial subjectivity and freelance journalism in Sweden. Journalism, July* 2021, pp. 1–18. DOI: 10.1177/14648849211033131

NOU 2017: 7 Det norske mediemangfoldet. en styrket mediepolitikk for borgerne. Oslo: Official Norwegian Report [The Norwegian media diversity. A strengthened media policy for the citizens].

Nygren, G. (2008) *Yrke på glid: om journalistrollens de-professionalisering. (Profession on the slide – de- profesionalization of the journalistic role).* Stockholm: SIMO.

Nygren, G. (2014) Multiskilling in the newsroom: De-skilling or re-skilling of journalistic work? *The Journal of Media Innovations,* 1(2), pp. 76–96. DOI: https://doi.org/10.5617/jmi.v1i2.876

Nygren, G. and Boguslowa D.O. (2015) *Journalism in Change. Journalistic Culture in Poland, Russia and Sweden.* Frankfurt: Peter Lang Edition.

Olsen, K.S. (2018) *Tradisjonsforankrede og digitaldreide lokaljournalister. En hverdagssosiologisk studie av norsk lokaljournalistikk i en brytningstid.* Phddissertation. Bodø: Nord University [Traditionally Anchored and Digitally Oriented Local Journalists An Everyday Life-Sociological Study of Experiences and Tensions among Norwegian Local Journalists].

Örnebring, H. (2009) *The Two Professionalism of Journalism: Journalism and the Changing Context of Work.* Working paper. Oxford: Reuters Institute for the Study of Journalism. University of Oxford.

Örnebring, H. (2010) Technology and journalism as labour: historical perspectives. *Journalism,* 11(1), pp. 55–74. https://doi.org/10.1177/1464884909350644

Örnebring, H. (2018) Journalism and Change. In Vos, T.B. (eds.) *Journalism.* Mouton: De Gruyter, pp. 555–571.

Ottosen, R. (2015) Crisis or innovation? The Norwegian journalist between Market and Ideals in the Multimedia Era. In Maxwell, R. (ed.) *The Routledge Companion to Labor and Media.* London: Routledge, pp. 202–217.

Peters, C. and Broersma, M. (eds.) (2013) *Rethinking Journalism. Trust and Participation in a Transformed News Landscape.* London: Routledge.

Peters, C. and Broersma, M. (eds.) (2017) *Rethinking Journalism Again. Societal Role and Public Relevance in a Digital Age.* London. Routledge.

Ryfe, D. (2019) The warp of woof of the field of journalism. *Digital Journalism,* 7(7), pp. 844–859. DOI: 10.1080/21670811.2018.1517605

Schudson, M. (2013) Would journalism please hold still!. In Peters, C. and Broersma, M. (eds.) *Rethinking Journalism. Trust and Participation in a Transformed News Landscape.* London: Routledge, pp. 191–199.

Sennett, R. (2008) *The Craftsman.* New Haven. Yale University Press.

Singer, J.B. (2017) The journalist as entrepreneur. In Peters, C. and Broersma, M. (eds.) (2013) *Rethinking Journalism. Trust and Participation in a Transformed News Landscape.* London: Routledge, pp.131–145.

Sjøvaag, H. (2019) *Journalism Between the State and the Market.* London: Routledge.

Skogerbø, E. and Karlsen, R. (2021) Media and politics in Norway. In Skogerbø, E., Ihlen, Ø., Kristensen, N.N. and Nord, L. (eds.) *Power, Communication and Politics in the Nordic Countries*. Gothenburg: Nordicom, pp. 91–113. DOI: 10.48335/9789188855299-5

Skogerbø, E., Ihlen, Ø., Kristensen, N.N. and Nord, L. (eds.) (2021) *Power, Communication and Politics in the Nordic Countries*. Gothenburg: Nordicom.

Skogerbø, E., Ihlen, Ø., Kristensen, N.N. and Nord, L. (2021) *Power, Communication, and Politics in the Nordic Countries*. Gothenburg: Nordicom, University of Gothenburg.

Sørensen, B. Aa., Seierstad, G. and Grimsmo, A. (2005) *Tatt av ordet*. Oslo: Arbeidsforskningsinstituttet. [Taken by the word].

Syvertsen, T., Enli, G., Mjøs, O.J. and Moe, H. (2014) *The Media Welfare State: Nordic Media in the Digital Era*. Michigan: The University of Michigan Press.

Wagemans, A., Witschge, T. og Deuze, M. (2016) Ideology as Rescource in Entrepreneurial Journalism. London: Routledge. DOI: 10.1080/17512786. 2015.1124732

Wahl-Jorgensen, K. and Hanitzsch, T. (2009) *The Handbook of Journalism Studies*. New York: Routledge.

Waisbord, S. (2013) *Reinventing Professionalism. Journalism and News in Global Perspective. Key Concepts in Journalism*. Cambridge: Polity Press.

Wiik, J. (2015) Internal boundaries: The stratification of the journalistic collective. In Carlson, M. and Lewis, S. (eds.) *Boundaries of Journalism. Professionalism, Practices and Participation*. London and New York: Routledge, pp. 118–133.

Zelizer, B. (2015) Term of choice; uncertainty, journalism and crisis. *Journal of Communication*, 65, pp. 888–908. DOI: 10.1111/jcom.12157

2 Journalism as a profession and institution

Birgit Røe Mathisen

Introduction

Journalism represents a societal institution with its own routinized practices and norms, as well as a profession consisting of humans performing this practice. The disruption of journalism can be analyzed from many angles, reflecting whether one's concern is with the news business as an industry, journalists as professionals, or the workflow of journalists. This volume is concerned with journalism as a profession rather than a business, industry, or news organization. However, the above-mentioned elements shape a vital framework that impacts on the environment where journalistic professional work is being conducted. Therefore, industrial aspects cannot be totally overlooked. This book focuses on three specific tensions within the profession of journalism, as discussed in Chapter 1: *pressures between precarity and autonomy, boundary disputes, and internal slides within the professional landscape.* This chapter lays out the theoretical groundwork and analytical foundation for the subsequent empirical chapters, discussing how the sociology of professions might help to understand the current disruption of journalism, as well as its impact on the institutional role of journalism. As such, it also draws upon institutional theory, and I open the theoretical discussion with a brief explanation of institutional theory, followed by the sociology of professions. Thereafter, I elaborate on vital concepts from this theoretical approach that are central in the following empirically based chapters.

Journalism as institution

As stated in Chapter 1, journalism as a societal institution plays a vital role in the public sphere and democracy. Consequently, to understand the current disruption of journalism, it is vital to gather knowledge beyond the mere professional perspective because it also has a societal and civic impact

DOI: 10.4324/9781003144724-2

on journalism's role in democracy and public discourse. Institutionalism is a widely recognized approach to the study of journalism (Ryfe, 2016, p. 370) and is a frequently used theoretical perspective that provides a useful lens through which to view the development of journalism (see, for example, Allern, 2001; Bjerke, 2009; Allern and Blach-Ørsten, 2011; Sjøvaag, 2018). Institutionalism is understood as the study of social identities and their rules (March and Olsen, 2004 p. 675; Ryfe, 2016, p. 370). Institutional theory underlines journalism as an institutionalized practice (Cook, 1998; Allern and Blach-Ørsten, 2011). Journalism is an independent part of society with its own norms and structures, and it is assigned a role within democracy (Cook, 1998; Sparrow, 1999). Consequently, journalism is given a specific kind of legitimacy, and news is a product with organizational expectations (Berkowitz, 2009). As McNair (1998, p. 62) states,

> The journalist is a professional communicator whose work is structured and shaped by a variety of practices, conventions and ethical norms as well as by the constraints and limitations imposed by the fact that journalism is a complex production process.

Journalism is defined by a shared set of organizational routines and practices (Ryfe, 2006, p. 135). Moreover, 'taken-for-granted-ness' is a key aspect of defining institutions, which suggests that value derives from widespread legitimacy and shared understanding (Lowrey, 2018, p. 127).

Anthony Giddens' structuration theory forms a vital ground for institutionalism in which institutions are 'the more enduring features of social life' (Giddens, 1984, p. 24). According to Giddens, a structure is a set of resources, rules, and institutionalized features out of time and space that are implicated in the production and reproduction of social practice. Structure organizes the social system, but it is not unchangeable. Giddens also emphasizes that human action and social structure are mutually dependent variables because they exist only in relation to each other. The duality of structure is also a core element: 'Structure is not to be equated with constraints but is always both constraining and enabling' (Giddens, 1984, p. 25).

Cook (1998, p. 70) defines institutions as 'social patterns of behaviour identifiable across organizations that are generally seen within a society to preside over a particular social sphere'. He underlines the similarities in the news-making process and the content of news across organizations, which justify the institution concept (p. 76). Cook also describes journalism as a collective process that is more influenced by routines and procedures than by the decisions of individual journalists. The institution shapes the journalists' behaviours over time (Ryfe, 2006, p. 138). Within the institution of journalism, the structure might be practiced as news values and professional norms that explain why journalists act as they do (Ottosen, 2004, p. 18). However, key aspects of institutions include their resistance to change and their durability (Ryfe, 2016, p. 370). Institutional scholarship might be accused of over-emphasizing stability and homogeneity (Lowrey, 2018, p. 136). This volume, like much of the scholarly literature, is focused on challenge and disruption. This justifies questioning the usability and relevance of a theoretical approach that highlights stability and resistance, which are quite the opposites of change.

According to Ryfe (2016), if institutionalism is to have a place in the study of digital journalism, we must demonstrate its capacity to explain both change and stability to 'capture the way in which old institutions are challenged or repudiated and new institutions are invented' (p. 371). He states that the most obvious path to change in journalism is via crisis or external shock. Examples of such external shocks might include the vanishing of an established business model and the rise of social media challenging journalists' gatekeeping role. These kinds of shocks are also called critical junctures. When a system experiences a shock, new opportunities may arise, followed by the creation of new institutional orders and a corresponding enhancement of stability. Fundamental change implies that new routines and practices emerge and develop (Ryfe, 2006, p. 138) and that they change how journalistic work is justified (Ryfe, 2016, p. 380). Thus, shocks and changes create a new form of stability – for the time being.

Another objection to an institutional approach to change might be raised based on the relationship between structure and actor. As professional work, journalism is associated with the concepts of having a mission, a calling, and a lifestyle (Bjerke et al., 2019, p. 16). Journalistic work thus represents a craft containing more artistic and creative aspects, and it calls upon the more individual aspects of each journalist. How does this fit an institutionalist and structuralist approach in which journalism is seen as a structure and journalists are considered collective actors with scarce and limited ability to influence the framework? The institutional approach has been criticized for over-emphasizing structure, stasis, and functionalist assumptions (Lowrey, 2018, p. 127). Giddens, however, emphasizes the mutual dependency of structure and actor. Following Giddens, Cook also highlights that news work both constrains and enables:

> And, to remember Gidden's analogy, just as speaking is both constrained by and adds to language, so newsmaking is both constrained by and adds to the rules and routines of journalism and contributes to their utility and perpetuation.
>
> (Cook, 1998, p. 76)

In other words, Cook (1998, p. 74) also acknowledges that journalists, despite the presence of routines, have available space in their day, and they both use discretion and improvise. Indeed, the need to improvise might be even clearer in uncertain times of rapid change, when old routines no longer provide suitable answers. Scholars have emphasized that the entrepreneurial competencies of innovation and adjustment are more necessary than ever as elements of the journalistic tool kit. Several schools of journalism have increased their focus on entrepreneurial skills as a way of preparing students for media work (Baines and Kennedy, 2010; Singer and Broersma, 2020) and to build an entrepreneurial mindset among students (Sparre and Færgemann, 2016). Entrepreneurialism explores opportunities to renew journalism. Where formerly strict boundaries between public service and business have become relaxed, they are now called to challenge traditional normative divisions. The crisis in the journalism industry has necessitated re-evaluation of the relationship between editorial and finance (Rafter, 2016, p. 140).

Lowrey (2018) discusses the institutional approach to contradictions as agency and structure, autonomy and constraints, and he emphasizes how journalism is conceptualized as an institution in various ways. One is as an organizationally bound enterprise with routinized practices, and another is as a meso-level collective field or space that has negotiated boundaries. The latter view appears in scholarship on journalism as a profession and represents attempts to accommodate not only agency and structure but also autonomy and constraints. Vital to the meso-level institutional approach is the notion that journalists inhabit a bounded collective space 'that allows journalists to develop a shared logic, to maintain some measure of independence, and to negotiate boundaries' (Lowrey, 2018, p. 135). Here, a vital perception is that journalists have structure and agency within such a space. Journalists are still influenced by external forces and seek accord with other dominant social institutions, but they have agency and can enact change and repositioning (Lowrey, 2018, p. 136). Institutionalism emphasizes the meaning of structure and routines, but it also acknowledges the importance of autonomy and the existence of a creative, discretionary space to a certain degree.

In particular, we focus on three aspects of institutionalism that constitute vital contributions to the understanding of changes to and the disruption of journalism as a profession. The first involves the societal role of journalism. Institutional theory highlights the role of journalism as a societal institution that both influences and is influenced by other institutions. As discussed in Chapter 1, journalism's increasing precariousness is also tied to an overall neoliberal shift affecting work life in general. Institutional theory helps to identify how overall societal processes and structural changes affect the working conditions of both an individual journalist at a tiny local newspaper located in a small rural community and a self-employed freelancer taking assignments for a diverse range of editors in the capital. Global processes and individual job experiences are interrelated. Institutional theory also functions as a useful lens for analyzing the civic consequences of these changes and examining how working conditions might affect the journalistic content that audiences are offered. For instance, are the journalists out in the field engaging in 'shoe-leather reporting' (Nygren, 2014), meeting people and reporting original stories, or are they 'chained to their desks' (Lee-Wright, 2012), doing desktop reporting, in which they communicate with sources via phone or social media and rewrite stories? What resources do journalists have available for investigative journalism, and how much time do they have for fact checking? Furthermore, how does the content they produce affect opinion-making processes and the public discourse that journalists facilitate?

The second aspect is the capacity to explain change by offering a tool for identifying critical junctures and external shocks and understanding their implications. Which aspects of journalistic work appear most resilient and unaffected by the shock, which new routines and practices arose from the critical junctures, how are changes justified, and what kind of new stability emerges?

The third is the bridge between structure and actor, where institutionalism acknowledges the profession's role (Cook, 1998, p. 77). Thus, the intersection of the institutional and professional aspects provides a useful lens for understanding the current state of journalism. The institutional logic might be viewed as a sense-making framework for engaging in daily activities, organizing time and space, and reproducing the experiences for those within the institution (Lowrey, 2018, p. 136). Within the institution of journalism, the profession comprises the actors who exercise, interpret, and implement procedures, routines, and practices (Mathisen, 2013). Here, we can identify a link between institutional theory and the theory of professions. As Waisbord (2013, p. 10) states,

> The study of professionalism highlights critical aspects of journalism as a societal institution: the formation and maintenance of occupational identities, the existence and challenges to consensus over journalistic work, the dynamics of autonomy and heteronomy vis a vis other fields, and the existence of a unique rationality – a journalistic logic that may set it apart from other actors and logics.

At the meso level, Lowrey includes Abbott's system of professions, which incorporates structure and agency. Professions reflect objective qualities as well as internal; the latter claiming the internal logic of the profession's claim of jurisdiction. Later in the chapter, I explore the sociology of professions, discuss journalism as profession, and elaborate upon vital concepts within this approach such as jurisdiction and boundary work. First, however, I address the question of whether journalism *is* a profession.

Journalism as a profession

As an academic discipline and educational field, journalism is a rather new subject. Journalistic work is performed in a constant state of tension between being part of a craft that demands practical and technological skills and being part of a profession that demands analytical reflection, theoretical insight, and broad societal understanding. This tension is sometimes expressed by practitioners and editors, who criticize researchers and journalism schools for being too academic and theoretical and for neglecting the practical and technological skills that journalists need to do their jobs. In contrast, academics argue that superficial coverage and clickbait journalism impair the public's trust, on which journalism depends to play its societal role as democratic infrastructure (Deuze, 2008). Being part of a profession gives individuals professional power in their work, and the profession as a whole exerts influence and power in society (Nygren, 2015, p. 21).

In the sociology of professions, three different concepts are widely utilized: profession, professionalization, and professionalism. These terms describe different aspects of professions, as explained by Evetts (2011, 2013). The concept of *profession* represents a distinct and generic category of occupational work, and it clarifies the differences between professions and other occupations (Evetts, 2013, p. 781). *Professionalization* describes the process by which an occupational group obtains professional status, and it has been interpreted as the process of pursuing, developing, and maintaining the closure of occupational groups (Evetts, 2013, p. 782). Here, maintaining occupational closure and jurisdiction are vital aims. In other words, this process defines the borders of the profession and controls who is allowed to be a part of it. Evetts described *professionalism* as an occupational and normative value system, as well as something worth preserving and promoting in work and by workers. Here, discretion becomes important. The concept of professionalism also includes a reassessment of the quality of professional performance and the construction of occupational identity (Evetts, 2011, 2013). This shared professional identity leads to similarities in work practices and procedures and shared methods of perceiving problems and solutions. This common identity is produced and reproduced through shared educational background, professional training, and membership in professional associations; together, these constitute a professional socialization process (Evetts, 2011, 2013, p. 780). 'In this way, the normative value system of professionalism in work, and how to behave, respond and advise, is reproduced at the micro-level in individual practitioners and in in their workplace' (Evetts, 2011, p. 780). Transferred to journalism, professional identity is produced and reproduced through socialization within the newsroom, journalism education, and journalists' professional associations or trade unions.

The concept of the profession represents a category of work that is distinct from other occupations. Within the theory of professions, the definition of profession has changed over time. Until the 1970s, the focus was to identify certain characteristics and classify professions according to these. These criteria are full-time work, formal education, professional organization, professional ethics, and a licence (Wilensky, in Bjerke, 2009, p. 59). Journalism meets some of these criteria but not all of them. It lacks authorization demands, a diploma, and licence protection. Journalism might even be characterized as a free occupation, as not even education in journalism is required to work as a journalist. However, journalism has an occupational ethical code, and the union constitutes a professional collective. Thus, several researchers have defined journalism as a semi-profession (Bjerke, 2009; Nygren, 2008, 2015; Ottosen, 2015). Freedom of speech is relevant, too, and neither the state nor occupational organizations shall control authorization demands regarding who can be defined as a journalist (Nygren, 2008, p. 16).

However, scholars such as Abbott (1988) and Freidson (2001) are more concerned with professionalization as power and control over knowledge than they are about categorization. A profession relies less on formal characteristics than on the belief that members of an occupation have a special status that enables them to exercise control over their own work. Thus, professionalism is a performed part of journalists' daily work (Cook, 1998, p. 77). Boundary work and jurisdiction become vital to defining the borders of journalism, where protecting professional autonomy is an essential aim. For journalists, the notion of public service and a degree of autonomy and control over work processes are essential to the professionalization process (Deuze, 2008; Nygren, 2015). Journalism is afforded the authority, privilege, and legitimization of a profession, but to maintain this status, it must depend on society to recognize its authority as necessary and legitimate. Thus, the question of whether journalism is regarded as a profession relates primarily to its societal role as an independent institution and a 'fourth estate' (Nygren, 2008, p. 167).

Controlling knowledge and skills

Freidson (2001, p. 17) sees professionalism as a set of institutions that permits the members of an occupation to make a living controlling their own work:

That is a position of considerable privilege. It cannot exist unless it is believed that the particular tasks they perform are so different from those of most workers that self-control is essential.

According to Abbott (1988, p. 8) professions are exclusive occupational groups that apply somewhat abstract knowledge to particular cases. He is concerned with how occupational groups control abstract knowledge and practical skills. He states, 'any occupation can obtain licensure or develop an ethics code. But only a knowledge system governed by abstractions can redefine its problems and tasks'. Abbott (p. 35) describes the relationship between professions and their work as complex because tasks, professions, and the links between them change continually. He describes several types of objective foundations for professional tasks (p. 39): technological, organizational, and natural objects and facts, as well as slow-changing cultural structures.

Abbott also states that research about professions has been more concerned with how they are organized than what they actually do, so structure has become more vital than practice and actual work in professions research. Freidson (2001, p. 23) discusses *discretionary specialization*: tasks in which discretion or fresh judgment must often be exercised if they are to be performed successfully. Workers must be prepared for individual circumstances that require discretionary judgment and action. He states, 'Such work has the potential for innovation and creativity'. Freidson relates discretionary specialization to both formal skills and tacit knowledge. In their daily work, journalists use discretionary specialization in a wide range of situations. For instance, they make judgments regarding whether a story is newsworthy or not, consider whom to interview and how to frame a story, make ethical considerations, decide which storytelling techniques to use, which platform is most suited to publishing the story, and how to use social media to distribute it (Olsen, 2018). In all these situations, there is no firm recipe or manual; instead, all individual journalists and the newsroom as a collective must use their professional discretion and draw upon tacit knowledge and formal skills. Returning to the institutional approach to journalism, Cook (1998, p. 74) also acknowledges that journalists use discretionary specialization, even if they are restricted by rules and structure.

Jurisdiction and boundary work

Professional control concerns jurisdiction and the identification of insiders and outsiders in a profession. Abbott (1988, p. 60) asserts that a jurisdictional claim generally concerns legitimate control over a particular kind of work, primarily the right to perform the work as professionals see fit:

They construct tasks into known 'professional problems' that are potential objects of action and further research. (…). In claiming jurisdiction,
a profession asks society to recognize its cognitive structure through
exclusive rights. (…).These claimed rights may include absolute
monopoly of practice and of public payments, rights of self-discipline
and of unconstrained payment, control over professional training, of
recruitment, of licensing to mention only a few.

(Abbott, 1988, p. 59)

Jurisdiction is a claim of both social and cultural authority. This concept
is closely related to the concept of boundary work, which Gieryn (1983,
p. 782) defines as 'the attribution of selected characteristics to the institution of science for purposes that distinguish some intellectual activities as
"non-science"'. The goal of boundary work might include the following:
expansion of authority into domains claimed by other professions, monop-
olization of professional authority by excluding rivals with labels such
as 'pseudo' or 'amateur', and protection of autonomy over professional
activities. Gieryn writes about science, but Matt Carlson has applied his
concept of boundary work to journalism by discussing how the boundaries
of journalism are constructed, challenged, reinforced, or erased. Boundary
work is about power: 'Being deemed a legitimate journalist accords prestige and credibility, but also access to news sources, audiences, funding,
legal rights and other institutionalized prerequisites' (Carlson, 2015, p.
2). Carlson states that journalism as a profession lacks firm borders, but
through boundary work, it strives for internal cohesion and the right to
reinforce its own exclusivity. Building upon Gieryn, he elaborates on how
boundary work might be used to understand the demarcation of journalism's norms, practices, and participants. Carlson discusses three types of
boundary work: *expansion*, which concerns incorporating non-traditional
journalists and expanding the borders of journalism; *expulsion*, which
entails expelling deviant forms and values (e.g., journalists who have been
faking stories and sources); and *protection of autonomy*, or preventing
non-professionals from influencing professionals' work and judgments.
Boundary work involves establishing borders that separate journalists from
non-journalists (participants), setting acceptable methods (practices), and
establishing journalism as a distinct community with specialized knowledge (professionalism).

Here, we might return to the Norwegian debate about union rules and
union membership for journalists, as discussed in the introduction of
Chapter 1. This debate might be understood as a typical boundary struggle
aiming to reinforce the borders of the journalistic community. The concerns
are whether the profession should expand and admit new groups or whether

the old borders should still be patrolled and guarded. A significant parallel is the heated debate that occurred in 1997 when the convention of the Norwegian Union of Journalists expelled all members working for PR firms and as heads of information departments in the private and public sectors. In total 150 members were expelled in a process defined by Ottosen (2015, p. 8) as a 'battle for the soul of journalism'. He elaborates that this 'was a classic example of how journalists tried to define their own (semi) profession by drawing a boundary against others'. Raaum (1999), a scholar of press ethics in Norway, characterizes the process as an 'ethical cleansing' and explains it as a symbolic act meant to define the identity of journalists. He states that the ethical norms of journalism are used to identify the territory and draw the boundaries between journalism and related work, such as information work. Furthermore, he considers ethical cleansing the most effective tool in the professionalization of journalism.

However, although the 1997 process resulted in the expulsion of members and narrowed the union's borders, the suggestion raised in 2020 concerns the opposite: expansion, or admitting new groups to the professional collective. The heated debate in 1997 constitutes a vital background for the protests that occurred 24 years later, and it is fundamental to the understanding of this new emotional debate. Through the lens of institutional theory, the 2020 suggestion regarding new membership rules might be interpreted as a reaction of critical junctures: economic losses and downsizing have led to a shrinking profession, and the trade union has lost 20 percent of its membership in recent years. The external framework has dealt the profession an impairing shock. Expanding the membership rules might create a new order and additional stability, but the protest also reveals how the proposal evokes a new boundary dispute aimed at protecting the soul of journalism and excluding other media workers. At the time of writing, the matter remains unresolved. The union is preparing for a broad debate among its members, and it will make the final decision at a convention in spring 2023.

Of journalists, Abbott (1988, p. 225) states, 'the incumbent profession of journalism has come to extraordinary power', through the steady growth of its jurisdiction in size and importance throughout the 20th century. However, Abbott describes journalism as a permeable occupation because mobility between journalism and PR and between journalism and other forms of writing is quite common.

> While there are schools, associations, degrees and ethics codes, there is no exclusion of those who lack them. (…) What matters is that interprofessional competition in fact shaped it decisively.
>
> (Abbott, 1988, p. 225)

Journalism navigates a changing world and confronts doubts about its future, so it is important to understand its unique position as it strives to maintain autonomy from external forces. 'This is why professionalism understood as collective efforts to set up boundaries to exercise jurisdictional control remains relevant' (Waisbord, 2013, p. 10). Autonomy is essential for a profession to exert full control over a certain jurisdiction (Abbot, 1988; Waisbord, 2013), so it is a key concept within the sociology of professions. The discourse about disruption and challenge of journalism is often tied to autonomy and a fear that journalism will evolve such that professional control is weakened and autonomy becomes poorer. Below, I discuss the concept of autonomy before addressing whether the changes lead to a professionalization or de-professionalization of journalism.

Autonomy

Historically, the notion of autonomy has been central to the ideals of journalism, and it remains a core ideal in the standard model of professional journalism. Autonomy is necessary for a profession to exert full control over a certain jurisdiction (Abbott, 1988). Conventionally, journalism has been expected to remain autonomous from businesses, political parties, and publishers if it is to serve democracy (Waisbord, 2013, p. 43). The value of autonomy is linked to the sovereignty of professions: the right to self-rule and self-government, as well as the right to exercise the profession's own logic, make professional judgments, and employ discretion free of others' influence. The institutional approach discussed earlier in this chapter emphasizes that institutions must serve a public role. Autonomy is necessary when serving the public interest, and the notion of autonomy in journalism refers to the independence of institutions. Journalistic autonomy is linked to the need to control boundaries vis-à-vis external actors (Waisbord, 2013). In other words, the concept of autonomy addresses the profession's right to exercise discretion in its work based on the knowledge that defines the profession and to exclude other forces from these decisions. In addition, it is legitimized institutionally in the understanding of journalism's societal and institutional role. To be able to fulfil the independent role society assigns to journalism, professional autonomy is a prerequisite.

Professionalism is also a political process through which the profession's actors seek power and privilege. Journalism's most vital argument for professional power relates to independence. Bjerke (2009) shed critical light upon the professional power and ideology of journalism, which he finds lacking in societal legitimacy. He defines the core of the journalistic professional ideology as the idea that journalism should be controlled by journalists only, and journalists should only be led by their peers (2009, p. 401).

Autonomy is also regarded as a building block of journalists' professional identity (Deuze, 2008, p. 448). Scholars describe the professionalization of journalism as a distinct ideological development or process in which the ideology continuously defines and redefines what constitutes consensus about what 'real journalism' is and who is regarded as a 'real journalist' (see, for example, Zelizer, 2004).

Deuze (2008) discusses the professionalization of journalism as a consolidation of a consensual occupational ideology, in which ideology is seen as a system of characteristic beliefs, including group meaning-making and idea generation processes. Autonomy is essential to professional identity and ideology, as journalists claim an exclusive role and status in society. This autonomy is about freeing professional judgments from interference from public criticism, corporate ownership, or marketing (Deuze, 2008, p. 448).

Professionalism or de-professionalization?

Evetts (2013, p. 784) states that the discourse of professionalism can be analyzed as a powerful instrument of occupational change and social control at the macro, meso and micro levels. She discusses three interpretations of professionalism. The first is occupational professionalism, which entails collegial authority, discretion, and occupational control of the work, as well as professional ethics monitored by institutions and associations. The idea of autonomy makes professionalism attractive to aspiring occupational groups. This rather positive or optimistic interpretation is based on the principle that the work is important to the public. The second is organizational professionalism, which is based on rational and legal forms of authority, standardized procedures, and increasing managerial control over work: 'It relies on externalized forms of regulation and accountability measures such as target-setting and performance review' (Evetts, 2013, p. 787). This is a more pessimistic interpretation of professionalism, which is seen as a process of implementing market closure, managerial control, and hierarchical structures. Third, Evetts discusses professionalism as mechanism for facilitating and promoting occupational change, a combination of the two previously described interpretations:

> The meaning of professionalism is not fixed, however, and sociological analysis of the concept has demonstrated changes over time both in interpretation and function. All of these different interpretations are now needed to understand the appeal of professionalism in new and old occupation, and how the concept is being used to promote and facilitate occupational change.
>
> (Evetts, 2013, p. 790)

The concept of the *division of labour* (Freidson, 2001) represents the organization and coordination of the relations between workers engaged in different but interconnected specializations. To make sense of this division, one must specify the source of the power that shapes it (2001, p. 41). Freidson defines three logics for controlling knowledge-based work such as journalism: *free market control, bureaucratic control*, and *occupational control*. The occupation division involves work that is controlled by workers themselves rather than consumers and managers. This exists today in crafts and professions, though never in ideal or typical form, according to Freidson (2001, p. 52). This occupational controlled division of labour is an essential part of professionalism: 'Specializations are stabilized as distinct occupations whose members have the exclusive right to perform the tasks connected with them' (Freidson, 2001, p. 56).

These kinds of ideal logics are always mixed, but the model makes it possible to discuss what kind of logic dominates the development and what gains the most power in daily work. Abbott states that a profession is always vulnerable to changes in the objective character of its central tasks (Abbott, 1988, p. 39). A vital discussion concerns which forces drive the changes and control the development, as well as what logic gains the most control when journalism is challenged and disrupted. Also important is whether change and disruption in journalism lead to professionalization or de-professionalization.

The Swedish researcher Gunnar Nygren has discussed and elaborated on the development of and changes to journalism as a profession in several works (Nygren, 2008, 2014, 2015; Witschge and Nygren, 2009). Building on Freidson, Nygren argues that a vital question concerns which logic controls journalistic work: professional norms and discretions, the market and commercial values, or a bureaucratic logic dominated by laws and rules. He is also interested in whether professional logic or market logic is strongest (Nygren, 2008, p. 170). Nygren (2015, p. 23) also leans on Evetts, stating that journalism can be analyzed as an ongoing negotiation between the *organizational* demands of media companies' standards and goals and *occupational professionalism* – that is, the values, norms, and identities that journalists develop among themselves. Nygren distinguishes external and internal autonomy. External autonomy is freedom from pressure exerted by external forces and power in society, whereas internal autonomy concerns the position of journalists in relation to owners and marketing departments within media companies (Nygren, 2015, p. 29). Professional autonomy is difficult to measure, but it is under pressure from external challenges, according to Nygren.

In general, professions are subjected to social processes that undermine claims to autonomy (Freidson, 2001). For the most part, commercialism and bureaucratization have caused a loss of autonomy, and one might question the consequences for democracy. Social changes also force professions to redefine boundaries to preserve autonomy – that is, new boundary struggles emerge that are aimed at sustaining professional autonomy in new ways. An essential discussion is whether the changes and challenges threaten the autonomy in a way that leads to a de-professionalization. As Waisbord (2013, p. 59) states,

> The gutting of news rooms through slashed budgets and significant staff reductions has drastically changed working conditions. Increased pressures to deliver ratings mean that commercial expectations trump strict professional considerations (...). These changes have weakened the relatively stable conditions that once gave rise to the ideal of professional autonomy.

Nygren emphasizes that trends might both strengthen and weaken journalism. He discusses whether the changes in journalistic work such as the adoption of digital tools can be regarded as de-skilling or multiskilling. Based on a survey of 1500 journalists in Sweden, Poland, and Russia, he concludes that both statements are true:

> In general, multiskilling is more correctly defined as re-skilling and up-skilling. The new division of labor in journalism gives more room for creativity and more power to the individual journalist according to those with experience as multi-reporters. It gives more room for autonomy in their daily work, but at the same time multiskilling is also a strategy to increase efficiency and production in the newsrooms.
>
> (Nygren, 2014, p. 19)

On the one hand, multiskilling can give individual journalists more control over their work processes, but on the other hand, it also increases production demands and encourages desktop-based recycling work instead of engaging in shoe-leather reporting, getting out in the field, meeting people, and observing events. The labour market, with its outsourcing and downsizing, makes journalists more dependent upon editors, but it also makes it possible to choose where to publish and what content to work with.

Based on an analysis of Swedish and British journalists, Witschge and Nygren (2009) argue that two trends exist in parallel: a fading of professional values due to changes in the practice and a return to professional values. Journalism as a profession is getting weaker, which is an expression of de-professionalization. However, internally, journalists return to professional values when the profession is under external pressure:

When faced with economic and technological change and insecurity, it may be natural to reinforce basic values that are considered to be at the core of the profession.

(2009, p. 57)

Using professionalism as a framework and in-depth interviews as a method, the Norwegian scholars Hege Lamark and Lisbeth Morlandstø (2019) examine how changes in work affect how local journalists perceive their professional autonomy. Their study confirms the parallel trends discussed by Nygren (2014) and Witschge and Nygren (2009) in that the local journalists experience increased commercialization and a pressure to work quickly, are increasingly challenged by social media, experience more desktop work, and engage in less shoe-leather reporting. However, they still perceive autonomy in their work, make their own choices about what stories to work with to a certain degree, and prioritize shoe-leather reporting as much as they can. Lamark and Morlandstø (2019) conclude that there are clear de-professionalization tendencies in local journalism, but they also find clearer tendencies related to experienced autonomy compared to previous Norwegian studies.

Profession between stability and change

This tension between professionalization and de-professionalization also reflects the tension between doomsday scenarios and visions of hope in the scholarly literature, as well as the occupational perception of how journalism develops, as discussed in Chapter 1. It also constitutes a vital background for the tensions in journalism that this volume aims to discuss: *precarity and autonomy, boundary disputes, and internal shifts within the professional landscape.* In professionalism, autonomy is a principal value, and the essential question is which logic controls the work. Further, it addresses how external frameworks and forces influence the professional space and the relationship between structure and agency. Boundary struggles are vital to understanding how a profession is shaped and functions within its internal hierarchy. They explain how the demarcation lines are drawn, who is perceived as a journalist, and who is perceived to be outside the profession, as well as who is perceived to represent the core and centre and who is positioned at the professional periphery. In addition, as institutional forces also affect professional spaces, it is important to understand how the professional landscape slide relates to its own centre and periphery. These are the issues the following empirical chapters are intended to elaborate and discuss. Using institutional theory and the sociology of professions as theoretical lenses, they contribute to understanding how the journalism profession develops when facing disruption and resilience.

References

Abbott, A. (1988) *The System of Professions: An Essay on the Division of Expert Labor*. Chicago: University of Chicago Press.

Allern, S. (2001) *Flokkdyr på Løvebakken?* Oslo: Pax forlag [Herd animals in the national assembly?]

Allern, S. and Blach-Ørsten M (2011) The news media as a political institution. *Journalism Studies*, 12(1), pp. 92–105. DOI: 10.1080/1461670X.2010.511958

Baines, D. and Kennedy C. (2010) An education for independence. *Journalism Practice*, 4(1), pp. 97–113. DOI: 10.1080/17512780903391912

Berkowitz, D. (2009) Reporters and their sources. In Wahl-Jorgensen K. and Hanitzsch R.(eds.) *The Handbook of Journalism Studies*, Routledge, pp. 102–114.

Bjerke, P. (2009) *Refleks eller refleksjon? En sosiologisk analyse av journalistisk profesjonsmoral*. PhD-dissertation. Oslo: University of Oslo. [Reflex or reflection? A sociological analysis of journalists' professional moral].

Bjerke, P., Fonn, B.K. and Mathisen, B.R. (eds.) (2019) *Journalistikk, profesjon og endring* Stamsund: Orkana Akademisk. [Journalism, a profession in change]

Carlson, M. (2015) Introduction: The many boundaries of journalism. In Carlson, M. and Lewis, S. (eds.) *Boundaries of Journalism. Professionalism, Practices and Participation*. London and New York: Routledge, pp. 1–18.

Cook, T.E. (1998) *Governing with the News: The News Media as a Political Institution*. Chicago: University of Chicago Press.

Deuze, M. (2008) What is journalism? Professional identity and ideology of journalists reconsidered. *Journalism*, 6(4), pp. 442–464. London. Sage Publications. DOI: 10.1177/1464884905056815

Evetts, J. (2011) A new professionalism? Challenges and opportunities. *Current Sociology*, 59(4), pp. 406–422. DOI: 10.1177/0011392111402585

Evetts, J. (2013) Professionalism: Value and ideology. *Current Sociology Review*, 61(5–6), pp. 778–796. DOI: 10.1177/0011392113479316

Freidson, E. (2001) *Professionalism: The Third Logic*. Cambridge: Polity Press.

Giddens, A. (1984) *The Constitution of Society: Outline of the Theory of Structuration*. Cambridge: Polity Press.

Gieryn, T.F. (1983) Boundary work and the demarcation of science from non-science: strains and interests in professional ideologies of scientists. *American Sociological Review*, 48(6), pp. 781–795.

Lamark, H. and Morlandstø, L. (2019) Snakker journalister fortsatt med folk? In Bjerke, P., Fonn, B.K. and Mathisen, B.R. (eds.) *Journalistikk, profesjon og endring*. Stamsund: Orkana Akademisk. [Journalism, a profession in change].

Lee-Wright, P. (2012) The return of the Hephaestus: Journalists's work recrafted. In Lee-Wright, P., Philips, A. and Witschge, T. *Changing Journalism*. London: Routledge, pp. 21–40.

Lowrey, W. (2018) Journalism as institution. In Vos, T.P. (ed.) *Journalism*. Mouton: De Gruyter, pp. 126–148. DOI :10.1515/9781501500084-007

March, J.G. and Olsen, J.P. (2004) *The Logic of Appropriateness*. Oslo: ARENA, Centre for European Studies, University of Oslo.

Mathisen, B.R. (2013) *Gladsaker og suksesshistorier. En sosiologisk analyse av lokal næringslivsjournalistikk i spenning mellom lokalpatriotisme og granskningsoppdrag. [Positive stories about success. A sosiological analysis of local journalism in the tension between local patriotism and critical watchdog ideal]*. PhD dissertation. Bodø: Universitetet i Nordland.

McNair, B. (1998) *The Sociology of Journalism*. London: Bloomsbury.

Nygren, G. (2008) *Yrke på glid: om journalistrollens de-professionalisering. (Profession on the slide – de- professionalization of the journalistic role)*. Stockholm: SIMO.

Nygren, G. (2014) Multiskilling in the newsroom: De-skilling or re-skilling of journalistic work?. *The Journal of Media Innovations*, 1(2), pp. 76–96. DOI: https://doi.org/10.5617/jmi.v1i2.876.

Nygren, G. (2015) Professionalization, media development and comparative journalism studies. In Nygren, G. and Boguslowa D.O. (eds.) *Journalism in Change. Journalistic Culture in Poland, Russia and Sweden*. Frankfurt am Main: Peter Lang Edition, pp. 19–40.

Olsen, K.S. (2018) What we talk about when we talk about local journalism. Tacit knowledge during the digital shift. *Sur le journalism, About Journalism, Sobre Journalismo*, 7(2), pp. 126–139.

Ottosen, R. (2004) *I journalistikkens grenseland. Journalistrollen mellom marked og idealer*. Kristiansand: IJ-forlaget [At the borders of journalism. The journalist role between commerce and ideals]

Ottosen, R. (2015) Crisis or innovation? The Norwegian journalist between market and ideals in the multimedia era. In Maxwell, R. (ed.) *The Routledge Companion to Labor and Media*. London: Routledge, pp. 202–217.

Raaum, O. (1999) *Pressen er løs! Fronter i journalistenes faglige frigjøring*. Oslo: Pax Forlag [The press is loose. Fronts in journalists professional liberation].

Rafter, K. (2016) Introduction. *Journalism Practice*, 10(2), pp. 140–142. DOI: 10.1080/17512786.2015.1126014

Ryfe, D. (2006) Guest Editor's introduction: New institutionalism and the news. *Political Communication*, 23(2), pp. 135–144. DOI: 10.1080/10584600600728109

Ryfe, D. (2016) News institutions. In Witschge, T., Anderson, C.V., Domingo, D. and Hermida, A. (eds.) *The SAGE Handbook of Digital Journalism*. Los Angeles: SAGE.

Singer, J. and Broersma, M. (2020) Innovation and entrepreneurship: Journalism students' interpretive repertoires for a changing occupation. *Journalism Practice* 14(3), pp. 319–318. DOI:1080/17512786.2019.1602478

Sjøvaag, H. (2018) *Journalism between the State and the Market*. New York: Routledge.

Sparre, K. and Færgemann, H.M. (2016) Towards a broader conception of entrepreneurial journalism education. Starting with everyday practice. *Journalism Practice*, 10(2), pp. 266–285. DOI:10.1080.1751286.2015.1123110

Sparrow, B.H. (1999) *Uncertain Guardians: The News Media as a Political Institution*. Baltimore: Johns Hopkins University Press.

Waisbord, S. (2013) *Re-inventing Professionalism. Journalism and News in Global Perspective. Key Concepts in Journalism.* Cambridge: Polity Press.

Witschge, T. and Nygren G. (2009) Journalism: A profession under pressure? *Journal of Media Business Studies*, 6(1), pp. 37–59. ISSN 16522354 [Article]: Goldsmiths Research Online.

Zelizer, B. (2004) *Taking Journalism Seriously: News and the Academy.* Thousand Oaks: Sage.

3 A shifting professional landscape

Paul Bjerke, Birgitte Kjos Fonn, and Birgit Røe Mathisen

Introduction

The professional journalistic landscape is in transition, reflecting the impact of several distinct features prompting change. The transition is dual edged. On the one hand, it leads to disruption, as well as a decrease in and a weakening of the profession as journalistic agenda-setting power crumbles. On the other, however, there is evidence of the rise of a new form of professionalism, as the internal hierarchy shifts and newcomers enter the field.

One distinctive feature of the landscape is that the overall number of journalists has decreased as a result of downsizing and cutbacks in traditional newsrooms across recent years (see, for example, Cohen, 2019). Downsizing and closure lead to a more challenging workload for the remaining staff. This development was described in other European countries already more than a decade ago (Franklin and Carlson, 2011) and struck Norway in full a few years later. In parallel, technological developments have led to a heightened focus on metrics and audience traffic, which have become exceedingly decisive forces affecting journalistic professional judgments and discretions, and blurring the barrier between professional judgments and commercial considerations (Cohen, 2019). Scholars have expressed concerns as to whether beat reporting (or specialized reporting) is under pressure with the renewal of the general journalist profile, or 'all-rounder' (Van Leuven, Vanhaelwyn, and Raeymaeckers, 2021). Social media has also contributed to making the demarcation line between journalism and related text forms less clear, and the boundaries of journalism are challenged both from the inside and the outside. Revenues fall drastically and, in many ways, we might state that the traditional media business shrinks and loses ground. At the same time, new start-ups are being established, and journalistic work is taking place in a diversity of forms and organizations.

DOI: 10.4324/9781003144724-3

This chapter aims to describe and discuss what we perceive to be a shifting professional landscape, where the internal hierarchy in the profession might change, and where blurred boundaries might challenge what we define as journalism and who are considered journalists. The chapter is co-authored by three researchers who have investigated the profession of journalism for several years and contains two main empirical parts. In the first, we describe structural trends and developments in the profession of journalism in Norway, including an attempt to map the emerging journalistic field. We also draw upon former theoretical and empirical work.

The second part is based on recent interviews with journalists that all work outside the traditional, larger newsrooms that have typically been subject to the main interest in scholarly research, aiming to discuss professional identity, motivations, and professional self-perceptions. What the interviewees have in common is that they work in media in the periphery or on the 'fringes' of the established – in everything from new hyperlocal outlets to trade or culture magazines that have changed their modus operandi. The concept 'fringe media' is often used to describe fanzines. We define it more generally, as outlets on the fringe or peripheral parts of the media landscape.

Data and methods

The chapter is partly based on a preliminary mapping previously published in the Norwegian language only (Fonn et al., 2019), aiming to offer a typology of the emerging landscape of fringe outlets in Norway. Recently, this study was followed up and extended with research focusing on the effects and legitimacy of the government's press support scheme, which both contributes to an understanding of how around 30 editors, politicians, scholars, and other experts and press organizations' representatives view the current situation, as well as a mapping of hyperlocal start-ups.

It must be said that for the time being it is difficult to try to give qualified figures, as publications come and go at considerable speed (see e.g., Høst, 2021). Our aim, however, is not to quantify any trends but to discuss how various kinds of fringe media relate to the profession of journalism.

Why is such a mapping of publications of relevance in a volume focusing on journalism as a profession rather than media as business or industry? One reason is that they represent both professional possibilities and a workplace for journalists. Another is that aspects of business and industry always constitute a vital framework for the profession. The mapping contributes to an overview of where journalistic work is conducted and how the landscape develops. Within the institutional perspective, finance, technological development, and political decisions form the structure that is both constraining and enabling (Giddens, 1984, p. 25). As institutionalism might explain both change and stability (Ryfe, 2016), forces outside the newsroom must be taken into consideration when we discuss the profession of journalism. Such a mapping therefore sheds light on important trends that constitute the environment where professional identity is shaped within the context of the Nordic media welfare state, as discussed in Chapter 1 (see also Syvertsen et al., 2014).

The interview section contains qualitative interviews with six representatives of the new emerging journalistic landscape, either thematic or geographic. The informants were strategically selected in order to secure a range of experiences. We have included representatives of publications that are 1) a digital offspring of a technology magazine that has existed in print for years, 2) an online music magazine with a print precursor, 3) a relatively new local newspaper in print covering a small 'hyperlocal' area, 4) a new local online newspaper of considerable size, 5) a relatively new online political magazine, and 6) an online start-up focusing on law and judicial issues. The sample represents both founders and journalists employed in these outlets. With qualitative interviews as a method, we aimed to explore why they chose a career outside traditional newsrooms and how they perceive their professionalism. The interviews were conducted across spring and autumn 2021 using a video link. Interviews were transcribed and thereafter analyzed by the three authors together.

Diversity and concentration of ownership

Before we proceed, it is important to take a look at how the Norwegian media field is placed between the state and the market (Sjøvaag, 2019), supported by an active media policy concerned with the democratic role of journalism (a 'media welfare state' (Syvertsen et al., 2014); see also Chapter 1), but it is still experiencing disruptive forces and neoliberalist flows. Thus, exploring the development within this national context will add valuable knowledge to the understanding of journalism as a profession.

The Nordic countries – Finland, Sweden, and Norway – are ranked highly in terms of printed newspaper circulation per 1,000 inhabitants (Lindén et al., 2021, p. 157). The media policy includes press subsidies to contribute to and strengthen media diversity. Subsidies are crucial both for supporting a smaller set of niche publications and the larger number of local newspapers. As we will see, an active culture policy also plays a role in the emerging landscape.

The greater number of news outlets is still in print (including digital versions), and, despite the fact that online papers have slowly taken over, there has not been any wave of newspaper closures, not even in 2020 with the problems flowing from the COVID-19 pandemic (Høst, 2021). This testifies to the considerable degree of diversity in the Norwegian press, but it must also be noted that the concentration of ownership in Norwegian media is fairly high, and increasing. By the end of 2020, the three major media companies owned almost 56 percent of the newspapers (Høst, 2021, p. 7).

The recent trend toward more concentration of ownership must however also be seen as a consequence of the ongoing crisis. Various calculations indicate that the total Norwegian media houses (the two national broadcasters TV2 and NRK not included) in the period 2008–2020 lost NOK 3.9 billion in revenue (NOK 5 billion in fixed 2008 kroner). The decline has occurred both in advertising and user revenue. The Norwegian Union of Journalists lost 20 percent of its members from 2011 to 2019 (Bjerke et al., 2019, p. 21). A significant proportion of the decline occurred in national newspapers (especially the single-copy newspapers) and regional media houses.

Although some of these effects have been compensated for by a harder pace of work for those still employed and more efficient digital work tools, there is no doubt that the ability to conduct journalism in various fields has deteriorated, resulting in new media shadows or blind spots: i.e., geographical or subject/thematic areas that receive weaker journalistic coverage than desired (see e.g., Mathisen and Morlandstø, 2019; Halvorsen and Bjerke, 2019).

There could, however, be some light at the end of this particular tunnel. The news industry has succeeded in making greater numbers of readers pay for digital news: it should be noted that Norwegians are more positive about paying for online news than many other national communities (Lindén et al., 2021, p. 157; see also Høst, 2021).

The interviews with editors, politicians, scholars, etc. show that the situation is characterized by *relief* on the 'ground level' – for the first time for long, a larger number of new hires are being made. There are reports of a shortage of qualified journalists, especially in rural areas and small local newsrooms. At the corporate level and among independent observers, the perception is more reserved. The most important problem they highlight is that large parts of the news industry still receive the greater part of their revenue from the print edition – but trends signal that the paper edition is still losing ground. Many fear that when print circulation drops further, major advertisers that today choose print may disappear very quickly. Industry actors have experienced difficulty in moving advertisers to the digital arena. For journalists, this means that the 'new normal' of the labour market is instability.

Some of the informants believe that various parts of the industry are differently positioned. The Aller Group, for example, owns the daily newspaper

Dagbladet, several glossy weekly magazines, and some smaller websites. It is almost fully digital and says it will do well even if print disappears. By contrast, Amedia, Norway's largest group of local newspapers, is probably in a worse position, with many of its publications still reliant on large print-based circulations and advertising revenues.

Local journalists

A distinct characteristic of the Norwegian media landscape is its decentralized structure, with a wide range of local, hyperlocal, and regional editions throughout the country (Syvertsen et al., 2014). Despite cutbacks and downsizing, local press remains crucially important (Syvertsen et al., 2014, p. 55). Local media structures have also remained remarkably stable despite technological and economic shifts and disruptions, indicating that localism, one of Norwegian society's deepest structures, may be a characteristic of the Norwegian media structure in the foreseeable future (Skogerbø and Karlsen, 2021, p. 99).

Local media is regarded as a significant 'glue' in local communities (Mathisen, 2013; Nielsen, 2015). Local journalists perceive their societal mission to be dual and to some extent contrasting and opposing. On the one hand, local media fulfil professional ideals and ambitions concerning critical, independent, and investigative journalism, which are also at the core of the professional ideology of journalism. On the other, they meet expectations to act as patriotic cheerleaders, supporting local communities and local institutions, and contributing to identity and a sense of belonging (Mathisen, 2013, p. 7). The role of local journalists can also be described as a tension between loyalty to the profession and the professional ideals of journalism but additionally a similar loyalty to the community (Mathisen, 2013, p. 109). In a disrupted and digitized media environment, local journalists are also located in the tension between tradition and innovation, stability or change. Olsen (2018) describes local journalists as two contrasting ideal types: the traditionally anchored journalist on the one hand, underlining a critical and autonomous role and societal mission, and the digitally oriented journalist on the other, who is more dedicated to audience choices and metrics.

In the past, local journalism has received little scholarly attention (Wahl-Jorgensen and Hanitzsch, 2009), but recent media research has valued and discussed the societal role of local journalism and recognized its value (Nielsen, 2015; Hess and Waller, 2017; Waskhova Císařová, 2017; Mathisen and Morlandstø, 2019; Gumera et al., 2018; Olsen, 2018; Mathisen, 2021). This increased scholarly interest embraces a variety of aspects, such as the role of local journalism in the digital media landscape, as well as the work and practice of local journalists.

According to Hovden's (2008) description of the journalistic field discussed in Chapter 1, local journalists used to suffer from a relatively low professional prestige, and local journalists certainly express a feeling of inferiority or lack of professional capital compared to colleagues in larger newsrooms. However, they also protest and underline that professional norms and values differ in various types of newsrooms (Mathisen, 2013, p. 92).

Based on an interview study with Norwegian local journalists, Lamark and Morlandstø (2019) conclude that they have obtained and enforced professional autonomy. Local journalists go into their communities and conduct shoe-leather reporting (Nygren, 2014, p. 20) rather than being chained to their desks (Lamark and Morlandstø, 2019, p. 231). Despite downsizing and more intensified work in the newsrooms, they describe a development toward increased job satisfaction and professional empowerment. Local journalists also enjoy a high score concerning public trust. Proximity to their community, local institutions, and sources also entail trust, as well as ease of access to institutions and sources (Mathisen, 2021), which again constitute a vital value in the professional role of local journalists.

Blind spots and new hyperlocal media

Despite this decentralized structure, the last years have seen a surge in new local and hyperlocal media. One reason is that regional media have downsized and prioritized coverage of the more central parts of the region. Hyperlocal media are geography-based, community-oriented, and native news-reporting organizations indigenous to the web, which are intended to fill perceived gaps in the coverage of an issue or region and to promote civic engagement (Metzger et al., 2011, p. 774). Recent research (Mathisen and Morlandstø, 2019; Halvorsen and Bjerke, 2019) has indicated that a result of the media crisis has been the development and growth of local and thematic journalistic blind zones, that is areas of society being sparsely covered by journalists. Even central parts of the country have suffered from particularly 'thin' local coverage, including the capital Oslo and its surroundings (Mathisen and Morlandstø, 2019).

Since June 2021, there seems to be a total of 35 functioning professional local digital news websites that are not based on 'old' legacy newspapers. Amedia has, for example, launched large local online newspapers in a few of Norway's largest cities. Some smaller titles have also proved popular and have become part of the established journalistic field and have already been included in the system of government subsidies after only a few years in business. This kind of start-up entails professional possibilities for journalists, as they both exceed and sustain local journalism. Several of the start-ups, however, have proved unstable and short-lived, a trend suggested in a range of countries (Kerkhover and Bakker, 2014; Williams and Harte, 2016). Still, they may represent vital democratic functions throughout extensive coverage of local politics (Williams, Harte, and Turner, 2015).

In political documents, geographic blind spots have been problematized, whereas the thematic blind spots have been less frequently addressed. Sjøvaag and Pedersen (2018) stress that blind spots that are also thematic have emerged after the newsrooms' downsizing took effect. Topics like working life, climate, immigration, religion, and the oil industry are only sparsely covered in local media (Mathisen and Morlandstø, 2019), whereas topics ranging from foreign news via economic questions to culture seem to be under-covered in national media as well (Fonn et al., 2019).

The trade press

An overview of Norwegian journalism at the beginning of the 2020s must also take the specialized press into account, including a number of newspapers/ magazines for organizations, trade unions, special activities, and so on. These national thematic niche outlets share several structural similarities with the local press. Historically, the trade press did not differ much from the daily press; the dividing lines were drawn much later when the daily press slowly became professionalized, first within the realms of the party press and, from the 1970s, in the realm of a commercial press. In later decades, the trade press, through its common association called 'Fagpressen' (The Trade Press), has gone through a significant professionalization process, not least by insisting on editorial freedom and adopting the same ethical framework as the established news press. Their increasing professional awareness has also been enhanced by the introduction of special prizes for this part of the press, which is associated with high prestige and often awarded to major investigative projects. In parallel, a significant amount of the trade press has established its own online editions, or new ones have been launched online (Fonn et al., 2019, p. 73 ff.). The landscape has been changed by the fact that traditional paper-based trade publications have become digital and thereby appear in the same news cycle, in social media and elsewhere, as the legacy news media, and that new outlets appear and seek membership in Fagpressen.

The result is that the boundaries between news media and the trade press are again exceedingly blurred. This media strand is essentially doing well and is increasingly, both legally and professionally, equated with the traditional news media. The trade press is also less susceptible to competition from free media and other entertainment media than are traditional newspapers. The trade press also has different means of financing compared to old news media and is therefore to a lesser degree negatively influenced by digitalization. Many are organizations owned and funded through membership fees and/or contributions from owners. The revenue loss is less dramatic, and they normally do not pay out dividends.

Almost half of the trade press publications in Norway (46%) describe themselves as *online newspapers with an emphasis on news dissemination.* This can be understood in light of the web's news-driving properties. This half has daily news updates on their websites and thus act as national news providers in their fields (Aker, 2020). The trade press has also increased its significance as an employer, regarding both journalistic quality and the number of jobs (Steensen and Kalsnes, 2020, p. 6). Examples of fairly new and successful trade press publications are *Medier24* (focussing on the media) and *Khrono* (focussing on higher education).

Culture journals

Culture journals are the third set of publications of interest to this study. One could argue that these have much in common with the trade press, with regard to their niche position, their financing, and the fact that many of them originate in print-based periodicals.

The culture journals however tend to be more programmatic, but could be about culture in both the wider and the narrower meaning. An example of a culture journal in the narrow sense of the word is *The Journal of Shakespeare and Theatre*, whereas a number of debate journals cover societal culture more widely.

The main difference is that while trade press members are part and parcel of an organization, and over the last 20-odd years have worked hard to professionalize their activities as *journalism* by increasingly adopting professional journalistic norms, culture journals are often identifiable by the fact that they do not regard themselves as journalistic. They have weaker or little journalistic self-perception, and this has also been apparent in their preferred use of genre; however, although the news story is the most common genre in the established journalistic media, the essay has been more common in culture journals (Bjerke and Halvorsen, 2018, p. 55).

In recent years, however, an increasing number of culture journals have become digitalized. Some have parallel print and digital issues, and some have become digital only. This has led to important changes in the *form* of many culture journals. Digital publishing repeals the former publishing rhythm, resulting in several culture journals resorting to publishing *news*.

They thus acquire a more journalism-like form, and their activities become closer to or even *become* journalism.

So, how does one draw the line? Bjerke and Halvorsen (2018, p. 13), in a study about the culture journals in Norway, found one decisive criterion: that they received financial support from the Arts Council Norway. This is, of course, a technical definition – it means that the council has, at an earlier stage, found these publications to fulfil a need in the culture sector, that they have been of some quality, and that they were subsequently worthy of some support. Apart from the fact that this definition – at least so far – has been helpful in drawing some lines, it also shows that Norway's relatively successful cultural policy may have contributed to the diversity we see today.

Subsequently, in the cultural field, previously printed journals create websites or become purely digital news sites and assume a journalistic or journalism-like format. The landscape is further complicated by the fact that at the same time, some of these boundaries have also been unclear in the past.

Crossing internal lines

As we have seen, the diverse landscape contains a range of thematic start-ups. They all seek to fill 'empty niches' in the media ecology by identifying thematic blind spots. Some have already sought admission to the trade press association, whereas others have not or may feel that this is not where they belong.

Among these, there are a number of new websites with a more significant political profile and newspaper ambitions. Since the dissolution of the party press that roughly took place between the 1970s and 1990s, objectivity has generally been accepted as a journalistic norm in Norway. There has, however, always been a small set of political newspapers that have also been supported through the system of press subsidies for the sake of diversity.

The newcomers generally tend to gravitate towards the press organizations and even the system of press subsidies, and a political inclination is no obstacle to this, despite the enduring focus on objectivity. Among the digital newcomers, a conservative paper (*Minerva*) is already fully accepted in the profession as a recipient of governmental financial support and membership in the press organizations. Others are more contentious. The editors of two new right-wing papers (typical 'alternative media') are a case in point: one has been accepted as a member of the Norwegian Editors' Association, whereas the other's application has been rejected twice.

There is also a certain degree of 'internal' border-crossing behaviour. We can see that from a tendency to change organizational affiliation. The conservative paper *Minerva* mentioned above is the obvious example in this regard. Formerly a cultural journal, established in the 1950s, it was recently partly financed by the Arts Council Norway, but it has now become a digital news and opinion site – and has recently started to receive press subsidies as well. Others have gone from weekly magazines to trade press to digital newspapers in little more than a decade; one example is the business site E24. This border-crossing behaviour, in which outlets not only cross the line separating those 'inside' and 'outside' journalism's professional structure, but also cross this structure's internal (often porous) borders, contributes to the complexity of determining what journalism is and who we define as journalists, and also to the shift in the hierarchy.

Media policy and the presence of solid professional associations and unions obviously have many effects. For instance, these factors might explain why there are many fringe outlets, as these factors might make it attractive to gravitate towards journalism's formal structures, and they might make newcomers more attentive to journalism's values and code of ethics. At any rate, these new publications represent new professional possibilities in which journalism can take a variety of forms, and organizations can be perceived as unique laboratories for new forms of journalism (Bruno and Nielsen, 2012). To understand contemporary journalism, knowledge about its direction outside the traditional mainstream newsrooms is fundamentally important (Iversen, 2020, p. 196).

Newcomers to the field

This trend raises interesting questions regarding how it contributes to the shifting professional landscape. What characterizes professional identity and self-perception among newcomers to the field? This brings us to the second empirical part of the research: the interview study among founders and journalists in journalism start-ups. None of our interviewees work in a traditional newsroom. Instead, they have been sampled because they have chosen a divergent professional career. We focus on discussing these individuals' professional identities and values, their motivations, whether they experience autonomy in their work, and how they perceive their role in a wider, more diversified media ecology. We begin by describing their background and their professional identity.

Background and affiliation

The six informants differ in terms of background. Two of them were educated at journalism schools, and three of them possess university degrees (among them, one majored in film studies). Many have 'signed on' to journalism. One interviewee dropped out of high school after one year because he preferred working with the newspaper. Two had their journalism debuts as teenagers in local newspapers. As one explained, 'I'd wanted to be a journalist since I created a school newspaper in elementary school, so I simply called the editor of the local newspaper'. Several informants took breaks from their journalism careers. One changed careers from the publishing industry to journalism in adulthood, but s/he considered becoming a journalist when s/he was younger.

Journalism has never been a 'closed shop' profession with educational requirements. In Norway, journalism school has become the most common form of education for journalists in recent decades (Fonn, 2015, p. 268 ff.), but it remains an open profession with many recruitment paths, as reflected by our informants.

Several informants have considerable experience from general and mainstream media. One has 16 years of experience at one of Norway's major newspapers, one started as a desk editor in a medium-sized regional newspaper, another worked in one of Norway's largest radio channels for ten years, and yet another has seven years of experience from the trade press during the era when it was predominantly in print and published more infrequently. In addition, two of the informants come 'from the outside', as one started her/his own newspaper when still at school, and another changed career plans and started as a journalist just before s/he turned 40. From this, we can at least establish that fringe media do not primarily seem to be a recruitment channel for mainstream media (as, for example, the student media have been). At least some of the stream currently goes in the opposite direction.

Having common organizations is an important professional criterion (Bjerke, 2009). One sign of professional affiliation is that all of our informants are members of a professional organization. Two are members of the National Association of Norwegian Local Newspapers (Landslaget for lokalaviser, LLA), and one is also in the Association of Norwegian Editors. The other four belong to the Norwegian Union of Journalists. Admittedly, they are not particularly active in these organizations, and at the time of the interview, none held a formal position. They expressed interest in the organizations' course offerings, but they rarely used them. They justified this by saying they lacked the time, which hardly seems unreasonable: they all work in small or very small newsrooms – one is even alone in the newsroom – and consequently have little leeway. However, they pointed out the usefulness of meeting colleagues through professional organizations or unions.

Some informants are also in more informal contact with colleagues outside their own workplace. As one of them stated,

I can contact some of the editors in the biggest media outlets in Norway; I have worked extensively with them, and we can talk, so I'm a little privileged at that.

The informant with the least journalistic experience says that s/he is 'unsure of some journalistic matters', but that s/he is constantly learning – and s/he has a colleague with extensive experience from the daily press that s/he can ask for advice. In other words, the role model for his/her practice is the professional experienced journalist. In itself, this is a good example of how a newcomer enters the profession.

From this, we can conclude that our interviewees mostly perceive themselves unambiguously as part of this profession in terms of background, affiliation, and professional contact with colleagues. They value the professional collective, even if they lack time to use it more extensively.

Motivation

Throughout the interviews, we aimed to identify the motivation to enter fringe media or create new start-ups. One interviewee, a start-up editor, was working as a lawyer after having worked as a journalist for several years previously. S/he realized no outlet covered the judicial field to his/her satisfaction and estimated that a new publication might reach approximately 20,000 people educated in law. It turned out to be far more successful. This informant gave up a steady and well-paid job ('a foolishly well-paid job') to start a fringe paper. Another informant was 'a bit bored' at his/her workplace at the time and started wondering, 'is it not possible to do more with journalism?' S/he realized there was no proper local paper where s/he lived. 'I started to warm to the idea that maybe I could be the one to start a paper like that'. A fourth informant gave up traditional media to work with music whereas the fifth changed to journalism to work with political matters. The last offered the reason that is generally assumed to be the most common – downsizing in established media – but ended up writing about his/her original specialization.

In other words, we identified a tendency towards professional motivation to cover a specific niche or blind spot and to develop journalism in a certain direction. Such a motivation might be associated with altruism as a vital characteristic of professionalism (Nygren, 2008). These findings also correspond with former studies of journalistic entrepreneurs in that the motivation is rooted in a desire to create a kind of journalism that is lacking in mainstream media or to fill in a blind spot (Iversen, 2020).

Professional values

From motivation, we move on to how the informants perceive the values of journalism. When it comes to professional values, there seems to be little difference between fringe staff and journalists in legacy media. Our informants prioritize journalistic values such as taking a critical stance and pursuing enlightenment, fairness, and truth.

A core point in journalism practice is news orientation. News, as the main genre of the trade, differentiates journalism from other kinds of non-fiction writing such as periodicals and non-fiction books. Almost all our informants talked about news and its importance in their work. They related to the news and the news flow. The only exception was the informant with the shortest journalism experience. S/he works in a publication that mostly publishes opinion pieces and some interviews – normally not news. However, in her/his experience, they are very much part of the common news cycle:

> We are particularly satisfied with a text if it ends up on [one of the three most important broadcast debate programmes]. Then we've contributed to setting the agenda.

In addition to those 'high' values upon which all journalists – and codes of ethics – agree, all mention the word 'engagement' or the ability to make readers interested. They ask themselves 'whether it is relevant, whether it is close, whether it is about some people you know already, whether it is a celebrity factor, but also such things as whether it engages a lot of people'. Another informant described it this way:

> Newsworthy for us is local, (…) preferably someone who has a sensational, funny, engaging story. And that we can take a good photo of them (…) Otherwise, you could say that it would also be newsworthy if we had a well-worked-out critical case.

A third informant even stated that there is no point in ignoring what is entertaining. Norwegian journalism has, in her/his view, long acknowledged

> entertainment or mirroring people's lives (…) if you are in what people perceive as the serious parts of journalism, then you often call it engaging. (…) I think it is rare that journalists produce pure entertainment without any social mission or information in it.

There is no doubt that news story selection is vitally important in journalism, and the ability to single out 'good stories' is often said to be the most important journalistic competence – but not at any price. One important point is the informants' concern for their community of readers, whether it be their local community, their trade, people with like-minded interests, or people with common political views:

> In a way, we consider our stories to be based on ordinary news criteria, but we always consider them based on the fact that we have an audience that is either very concerned about, or has life or work or an activity that is quite close to [our specialized field].

Even those with 20,000 or perhaps 100,000 readers (a high figure in Norway) emphasize that they create news – or debates – for a particular group:

> I think a lot of people have a feeling that this is 'their magazine', and it's also the key to success, creating an 'insider feeling'. They know that if they see that I use some slightly advanced expression in the ingress that is familiar to [my target group] but completely unknown to outsiders, then they feel that they are at home, and they feel like they're in.

A third emphasized that not being a 'clickbait newspaper' is liberating. 'We sell stories because people want to read them, but the important thing is that they will be read by the people who are interested in them'.

These answers illustrate unambiguously that the informants use ordinary journalistic news criteria but are very strongly audience oriented and interested in 'what my readers give attention to'.

Even though the informants differ in terms of background, and four have significant professional education in or knowledge about the field they cover, this does not mean they are all specialized beat reporters. Most are generalists in their field. One even stated clearly,

> I am a tabloid journalist. That's what they were looking for when they hired me, and that's definitely what they got.

Others think it is quite possible to be a specialized journalist without special knowledge and that it is sufficient to have journalistic knowledge and the willingness to dive into a field.

Our interviewees represent different types of journalists that have been identified in the established journalism literature and described in various research contributions, such as a comparison of the 'watchdog' and the 'entertainer' types (Hovden and Väliverronen, 2021; see also Olsen, 2018).

Here, we might conclude that the professional ideals remain strong, as also suggested by previous studies (Iversen, 2020). However, even if our informants obviously make typical journalistic news judgments, their news values differ to some degree and are tied more specifically to a targeted audience group or specific niche.

News criteria also differ between major mainstream papers, local papers, or 'traditional' niche papers. Thus, we might suggest that fringe media and newcomers contribute to widening the professional practice. The news judgments are drawn in a wide range of directions and contribute to more nuanced and multi-faceted professional judgments and discretion.

Autonomy

Many informants cite the fact that their job is often less click-driven than in general media and their closer relationship with their audience as reasons why they thrive and have opted out of mainstream media. Their main point was that working for a small, niche publication is better than working for traditional media: 'There is a huge freedom in being so small'.

Freedom was the most common notion among all informants. Most have found a kind of journalistic 'home' and meaning in conducting surveillance of their speciality. They believe working in fringe media – whether as leaders or employees – gives them a quite different sense of freedom compared to working in mainstream media. Even though this means lower salaries, as well as more worries, at least for those in charge of their outlet – they point out the indispensable value of the freedom to concentrate on what they find important. Thus, the respondents experience and value professional autonomy.

Several respondents expressed satisfaction when being able to contribute to the news flow in some way. None of them, however, were particularly eager to be first to publish breaking news. This is also something they have in common with many more established niche or local papers. They accept their position as 'minor players' in the field. They even see advantages to this, as they find themselves in a special position that benefits journalism and the public's access to information:

> In [a major daily] you may have to leave important stories because they are not broad enough, whereas we can come in as the little David [against Goliath] who fills the news out with something that, in the next round, can turn the whole thing over

Another pointed out the importance of a press that also reports small and seemingly unimportant stories:

> Some stories will never be written unless some people take on the task of doing those boring 'in-between' stories. It is only when you have

finished the first half-boring 40 'in-between' stories that you are in a position to write number 41. That is when you see the entire jigsaw puzzle.

Therefore, the crisis in mainstream media might have contributed to a richer media landscape and even a better service to the public. As one informant put it, 'I think that my field is not only better covered now than what it would have been without us, but also better than it was in the mainstream media's heyday'.

This is supported by how some of the respondents describe journalism as a community that exists across outlets, not just a pool of competitors. One said that if they come across a story that would be more suitable in mainstream outlets, they just give it to their friend. Another said that 'the others are not competitors, but colleagues', and a third that he likes the idea that 'we are really kind of competitors, but we also jointly inform the public'.

When discussing autonomy, the relationship with the owners is also of significance. Since the 1970s or 1980s, when the Norwegian party press began to dissolve, there has been a general perception that commercial owners and journalistic independence go hand in hand. However, the Norwegian media scholar Odd Raaum formulated: did independence from party owners really secure independent journalism? (1999, p. 166).

Half of the outlets in our study are owned by organizations. The others are truly independent – that is, they are start-ups and our interviewees are their founders, and the only way they can meet with their boss or board is by looking in the mirror. The founders also naturally feel that they have considerable freedom in terms of financial matters:

Perhaps the greatest freedom is that I can determine the editorial line for the newspaper and decide what I think is important.

Interestingly, however, those respondents working in publications that are organization-owned have the same feeling of autonomy. All three pointed out that the owners do not intrude with their editorial decisions. One also said that they are not dependent on clicks because they are fully financed by an organization. In the case of breaking news or debates, they are allowed to consider whether they want to follow up on the events: 'The fact that we are not commercial gives us freedom'.

This last informant works in a paper that is free and open. Another organization-owned paper is behind a paywall. This is quite an expensive profession-related paper, and the intention is that employers will subscribe to help their staff to stay informed. Price seems to be no obstacle, as this paper has the highest readership, but this does not mean that the income is profitable for anything other than the journalism: 'Our owners do not take any money out of the shop'. We have of course interviewed only a small number of media workers. However, the question of autonomy among media workers with organizational owners is of high importance in a changing journalistic landscape, so it should be a vital issue for further research.

Concluding remarks

In this chapter, we have described some trends in the Norwegian media landscape, as they constitute both the framework and professional possibilities for journalists. The professional landscape is subject to several kinds of changes, such as the downsizing of mainstream media and the ensuing decrease in the number of journalists. At the same time, the trade press and niche media have become more significant as employers, increasing their professional positions. New start-ups are established to cover thematic and geographic niches and blind spots. Local journalists in traditional small local newspapers experience increased interest and recognition and move closer towards the centre of the professional hierarchy. The interview study with six strategically selected informants representing newcomers indicates that they are motivated by the possibility of covering a niche and creating a kind of journalism that they find professionally satisfying. They identify themselves with and enter the profession, experience professional autonomy, and adhere to professional values. Still, they argue that they are in a better position to make divergent news judgments than mainstream media journalists. One should of course take into consideration that these kinds of arguments can be rooted in a need to position and legitimate oneself.

As beat reporting in general seems to have decreased due to downsizing, niche newcomers may nevertheless provide quality coverage that includes topic expertise and access to sources from different beats. In the interviews, our respondents described how they connect to their niche audiences, and they explained that the possibility of establishing this kind of relationship with readers who are genuinely interested in the same theme reduces click-bait and makes journalism more interesting and satisfying. They have a more loyal audience and some of them have safer funding. Consequently, the newcomers exceed the way professional discretions and judgments are conducted, and they draw journalism in a more multi-faceted direction. Similarly, the rise of newcomers in the field might reinforce occupational professionalism, as they contribute to journalistic norms, values, and identities (Evetts, 2013). They also sustain professional autonomy, which represents a core value of professionalism (Abbott, 1988).

However, newcomers may also suffer from financial uncertainty and a relatively fragile position (Williams and Harte, 2016). Even if they contribute to a shift in the landscape, their fragile positions might prevent them from advancing within the professional hierarchy. As founders of start-ups and entrepreneurs, they must juggle entrepreneurial values and journalistic professional ideals in a way that may make it difficult to distinguish what is regarded as journalism from what is not among these newcomers. Thus, it might exaggerate the blurred borders of journalism and lead to new boundary disputes that have the potential to disrupt the profession and make professional boundaries unclear. Consequently, societal trust in and recognition of journalism might suffer. If an increasing proportion of journalists work in single, small, fragile workplaces where the definition of journalism is unclear, such developments might lead to a de-professionalization rather than a re-professionalization.

These kinds of restrictions regarding newcomers and fringe media must be taken seriously when discussing their contribution to the journalism profession. Still, we find that they represent valuable contributions, and they are likely to reinforce professional autonomy and values. In the changing media landscape where mainstream media outlets are downsized and facing commercial demands, new niche media outlets exceed the available professional possibilities and might function as incubators and laboratories for developing new kinds of journalism. They contribute to a more diverse public by representing diverse voices and realities, offering in-depth coverage of thematic niches, societal questions or geographical areas that otherwise would have suffered from scarce coverage. In this way, newcomers might encourage public debate and reinforce how society acknowledges journalism as a vital part of democratic infrastructure.

References:

Abbott, A. (1988) *The System of Professions: An Essay on the Division of Expert Labor*. Chicago: University of Chicago Press.

Aker, T.K. (2020) *Fagpressen på nett (The trade press goes online)*. Master's thesis. Volda: Volda University College.

Bjerke, P. (2009) *Refleks eller refleksjon? En sosiologisk analyse av journalistisk profesjonsmoral*. PHD-disertation. Oslo: University of Oslo [Reflex or reflection? A sosiological analysis of journalists' professional moral].

Bjerke, P. and Halvorsen, L.J. (eds.) (2018) *Kulturtidsskriftene (The Cultural Journals)*. Bergen: Fagbokforlaget.

Bjerke, P., Fonn, B. K and Mathisen, B.R. (eds.) (2019) *Journalistikk, profesjon og endring* Stamsund: Orkana Akademisk. [Journalism, profession and change].

Bruno, N., and Nielsen, R.K. (2012) *Survival is Success: Journalistic Online Startups in Western Europe*. Reuters Institute for the Study of Journalism/ Challenges, Oxford.

Cohen, N. (2019) At work in the digital newsroom. *Digital Journalism*, 7(5), pp. 571–591. DOI: 10.1080/21670811.2017.1419821

Evetts, J. (2013) Professionalism: Value and ideology. *Current Sociology Review*, 61(5–6), pp. 778–796. DOI: 10.1177/0011392113479316

Fonn, B.K. (2015) *50 år med journalistutdanning. En historie om akademiseringen av et yrkesfag*. Oslo: Cappelen Damm Akademisk. [50 years of journalism education. A history of the academisation of a vocation].

Fonn, B.K., Bjerke, P., Knudsen, A.G. and Mathisen, B.R. (2019) Langt mer enn Akersgata: et nytt landskap tar form. [Far more than Fleet Street – a new landscape emerges]. In Bjerke, P., Fonn, B. K and Mathisen, B.R. (eds.) *Journalistikk, profesjon og endring*. Stamsund: Orkana Akademisk, pp. 65–89 [Journalism, profession and change].

Franklin, B. and Carlson, M. (2011) *Journalists, Sources and Credibility*. London: Routledge.

Giddens, A. (1984) *The Constitution of Society: Outline of the Theory of Structuration*. Cambridge: Polity Press.

Gumera, J.A., Domingo, D. and Williams, A. (2018) Local Journalism in Europe: Reuniting with its audiences. *Sur le journalisme, About journalism, Sobre journalism*, 7(2), pp. 4–10. https://doi.org/10.25200/SLJ.v7.n2.2018.353

Halvorsen, L.J. and Bjerke, P. (2019) All seats taken? Hyperlocal online media in strong print newspaper surroundings. *Nordicom Review*, 40(s2), 115–128.

Hess, K. and Waller, L. (2017) *Local Journalism in a Digital World*. London: Palgrave.

Hovden, J.F (2008) *Profane and sacred: a study of the Norwegian journalistic field*. Phd-thesis, University of Bergen.

Hovden, J.F. and Väliverronen, J. (2021) Nordic journalists' conceptual roles and perceived influences. *Nordicom Review*, 42(1), 141–161. DOI: 10.2478/ nor-2021-0034

Høst, S. (2021) *Avisåret 2020. Papiraviser og betalte nettaviser*. Report 108. Volda: Volda University College [The newspaper year 2020].

Iversen, B. (2020) Nye nettpublikasjoner, nye informasjonsstrømmer. [New digital publications and new streems of information]. In Ravnå, P.B, Mathisen, B.R. and Jorgensen, S.H (eds.) *Meningsdanning, deltakelse og kommunikasjon i demokratiske samfunn. [Opinionmaking, participation and communication in democratic societies]*. Stamsund: Orkana, pp. 195–218.

Kerkhoven, M. and Bakker, P. (2014) The hyper local in practice: innovation, creativity and diversity. *Digital Journalism*, 2(3), pp. 296–309. DOI: 10.1080/21670811.2014.900236

Lamark, H. and Morlandstø, L. (2019) Snakker journalister fortsatt med folk? In Bjerke, P., Fonn, B.K. and Mathisen, B.R. (eds.) *Journalistikk, profesjon og endring*. Stamsund: Orkana Akademisk. [Journalism, profession and change].

Lindén, C.G, Morlandstø, L. and Nygren, G. (2021) Local political communication in a hybrid media system. In Skogerbø, E., Ihlen, Ø., Kristensen, N.N. and Nord, L. (eds.) *Power, Communication and Politics in the Nordic Countries*. Gothenburg: Nordicom, pp. 155–174.

Mathisen, B.R. (2013) *Gladsaker og suksesshistorier. En sosiologisk analyse av lokal næringslivsjournalistikk i spenning mellom lokalpatriotisme og granskningsoppdrag. [Positive stories about success. A sociological analysis of local journalism in the tension between local patriotism and critical watchdog ideal]*. PhD dissertation. Bodø: Universitetet i Nordland.

Mathisen, B.R. (2021) Sourcing practice in local media: Diversity and media shadows. *Journalism Practice*, pp. 1–17. DOI: 10.1080/17512786.2021.1942147

Mathisen, B.R. & Morlandstø, L. (eds.) (2019) *Blindsoner og mangfold: en studie av lokaljournalistikken i lokale og regional medier*. Stamsund: Orkana Akademisk [Blind spots and diversity – a study of local journalism].

Metzgar, E.T., Kurpius, D.D., Rowley, K.M. (2011) Defining hyperlocal media: Proposing a framework for discussion. *New Media & Society*, 13(5), pp. 772–787. DOI: 10.1177/1461444810385095

Nielsen, R.K. (eds.) (2015) *Local Journalism. The Decline of Newspapers and the Rise of Digital Media*. London: I.B. Taurus.

Nygren, G. (2008) *Yrke på glid: om journalistrollens de-professionalisering. (Profession on the slide – de- profesionalization of the journalistic role)*. Stockholm: SIMO.

Nygren, G. (2014) Multiskilling in the Newsroom: De-skilling or Re-skilling of Journalistic work? *The Journal of Media Innovations*, 1(2), pp. 76–96. DOI: https://doi.org/10.5617/jmi.v1i2.876

Olsen, K.S. (2018) *Tradisjonsforankrede og digitaldreide lokaljournalister. En hverdagssosiologisk studie av norsk lokaljournalistikk i en brytningstid*. Phd-dissertation. Bodø: Nord University [Traditionally Anchored and Digitally Oriented Local Journalists. An Everyday Life-Sociological Study of Experiences and Tensions among Norwegian Local Journalists].

Raaum, O. (1999) *Pressen er løs! Fronter i journalistenes faglige frigjøring*. Oslo: Pax Forlag [The press is loose. Fronts in journalists professional liberation]

Ryfe, D. (2016) News institutions. In Witschge, T., Anderson, C.V., Domingo, D. and Hermida, A. (eds.) *The SAGE Handbook of Digital Journalism*. Los Angeles: SAGE.

Sjøvaag, H. (2019) *Journalism Between the State and the Market*. London: Routledge.

Sjøvaag, H. and Pedersen, T.A. (2018) The effect of direct press support on the diversity of news content in Norway. *Journal of Media Business Studies*, 15(4), pp. 300–316.

Skogerbø, E. and Karlsen, R. (2021) Media and politics in Norway. In Skogerbø, E., Ihlen, Ø., Kristensen, N.N. and Nord, L. (eds.) *Power, Communication and Politics in the Nordic Countries*. Gothenburg: Nordicom, pp. 91–113. DOI: 10.48335/9789188855299-5

Steensen, S. and Kalsnes, B. (2020) Fra fast lokaljournalist til midlertidig digitalt hode. *Norsk Medietidsskrift*, 27(1), pp. 1–20.

Syvertsen, T., Enli, G., Mjøs, O.J. & Moe, H. (2014) *The Media Welfare State: Nordic Media in the Digital Era*. Michigan: The University of Michigan Press.

Van Leuven, S., Vanhaelewyn, B. and Raeymaeckers, K. (2021) From one division of labor to the other: The relation between beat reporting, freelancing, and journalistic autonomy. *Journalism Practice*, pp. 1–20. DOI: 10.1080/17512786.2021.1910982

Wahl-Jorgensen, K. & Hanitzsch, T. (eds.) (2009) *The Handbook of Journalism Studies*. New York & London: Routledge.

Waschková Císařová, L. (2017) The voice of the locality. In Waschková Císařová, L. (ed.) *Voice of the Locality: Local Media and Local Audience*. Prague: Masaryk University, pp. 19–38.

Williams, A. and Harte, D. (2016) Hyperlocal news. In Witschge, T., Anderson, C.W, Domingdo, D and Hermida, A. (eds.) *The Sage Handbook of Digital Journalism*. London: SAGE.

Williams, A, Harte, D. and Turner, J (2015) The value of UK hyperlocal community news. *Digital Journalism*, 3(5), pp. 680–703. DOI: 10.1080/21670811.2014.965932

4 High job satisfaction and a precarious future

The double-edged nature of freelancing

Birgit Røe Mathisen and
Anders Graver Knudsen

Introduction

In journalism, a vital distinction is made between those professionals with permanent employment and those on temporary contracts or who work as freelancers. Throughout several countries, the number of employed journalists is shrinking, and the number of freelancers is growing, as the 2008 financial crisis led to wide-scale cutbacks and downsizing in newsrooms (Van Leuven, Vanhaelewyn, and Raeymaeckers, 2021, p. 2). Therefore, fewer journalists have permanent employment. The growth of individualized, contingent, and freelance work has led to a de-institutionalization of labour (Gollmitzer, 2020). Precarity has become part of the lived experiences of journalists, and these structural changes are part of broader societal trends towards individualization and job insecurity in neo-capitalism (Giddens, 2007; Sennet, 2008; Kalleberg, 2018). Sennet argues that the flexibility of the postmodern work-life balance makes it more individualized, resulting in uncertainty and confusion and undermining the feeling of responsibility for employees. Örnebring and Conill (2016) describe precarity as a key characteristic of contemporary journalistic work and argue that scholars should explain how precarity influences the ways journalists think about their profession. Scholars also discuss whether this rise leads to a de-professionalization of journalism in which professional values lose ground (Nygren, 2008) as the division between journalists with permanent contracts and freelancers intensifies. The European Federation of Journalists (EFJ) uses the term 'forced lancers', and although fewer permanently employed journalists are required to do more work, freelancers are used to fill the gaps, which make them vulnerable in the news industry (Van Leuven, Vanhaelewyn, and Raeymaeckers, 2021, p. 7). Cohen, Hunter, and O'Donnell (2019) found that most Canadian journalists laid

DOI: 10.4324/9781003144724-4

off between 2012 and 2014 moved from full-time work to more precarious forms of employment in and out of journalism, including freelance, part-time, and contract work. This development makes the working conditions of freelancers of fundamental interest when examining change and disruption in journalism and in the Nordic context (Norbäck, 2021). Although the Nordic model and the welfare state offer citizens relatively strong safety nets, as described in Chapter 1, Norwegian media work has also become more unstable and insecure reflecting downsizing and cutbacks in recent years. About 12 percent of the unionized journalists in Norway are freelancers (excluding students and pensioners). This proportion has been relatively stable, but it has increased somewhat in recent years.

Several previous studies describe the two-sided nature of freelance work and the contradictory experiences of autonomy and high job satisfaction on the one hand and precarity and vulnerability on the other (Gollmitzer, 2014; Cohen, 2016; Mathisen, 2016, 2018). This chapter sheds light on freelance journalists' working conditions based on a recent quantitative survey among Norwegian freelancers. The overall research question asked is: *what characterizes the working conditions of freelance journalists in the tension between precarity and autonomy?* This is a rather broad question, so to narrow our analysis, we elaborate in particular upon the experiences of freelancers working in investigative journalism and those taking assignments within the PR and communication fields. Investigative journalism is perceived as the core of professional practice, and it enjoys high professional prestige and recognition, whereas freelancers who combine journalism and PR work move into the blurred areas that are often subject to professional critique and that suffer low status. This situation also evokes boundary disputes. Furthermore, we take a closer look at those who consider leaving the media business and journalism, as this affects the future development of the journalism profession. The chapter is structured as follows: first, we present a literature review, including a discussion of the concept of freelancing. Then, we explain our data and methods before presenting and discussing our findings.

Literature review

A 2011 study conducted by the EFJ found that the proportion of freelancers and stringers in parts of central Europe was as high as 60 percent in some countries (Bittner, 2011). Freelance writing is a century-old practice dating back to the late 1500s (Massey and Elmore, 2018). Although it received little scholarly attention in the past (Wahl-Jorgensen and Hanitzsch, 2009, p. 12), in recent years, numerous studies have examined the professional role and working conditions of freelancers in the Nordic countries (Edström and Ladendorf, 2012; Ladendorf, 2012; Mathisen, 2016, 2018; Norbäck, 2021), other European countries (Gollmitzer, 2014; Hunter, 2016; Hayes and Silke, 2018; Marin-Sanchiz et al., 2021), Australia (Das, 2007; O'Donnell et al., 2016), and Canada (Cohen, 2016).

Journalistic work performed outside established newsrooms goes by various names. The International Federation of Journalists uses the term 'atypical workers' to describe relational types of employment that are neither regular nor full time (Walters et al., 2006, p. 6). This concept includes journalists on short-term rolling contracts, as well as those engaged in casual work, sub-contracted work, temporary work, and freelancing. Here, freelancing is perceived as a sub-category of atypical work and is defined as follows: 'typically self-employed, selling their services and work to a variety of employers without a long-term commitment to any of them' (p. 6). Stringers and correspondents are also included in this definition. The concept of freelancing often encompasses independent workers without permanent employment who take on individual assignments for several employers (Mathisen, 2016). As Cohen (2016, p. 9) claims,

Freelancers are self-employed workers who sell pieces of writing or contract their services to several media outlets without being employed by a single firm. In legal terms, freelancers contract for services with publishers, which means they are not hired, but only paid for work performed. (…). They have ongoing relationships with a number of clients in the same sector. (…). This arrangement situates freelancers outside traditional labour law and denies them the social benefits that are usually accessed through an employment relationship.

In this chapter, we rely on Cohen's description, and our study involves journalists who actively define themselves as freelancers through union membership and affinity.

Previous studies were concerned about job losses in journalism that forced journalists out of regular employment and into freelancing and short-term contracts (Cohen et al., 2019; Gollmitzer, 2020; Van Leuven et al., 2021). The core journalistic clientele is reduced, so many freelancers cannot live off their journalistic work alone and must take additional jobs, particularly in the PR field (Bittner, 2011, p. 11). Nygren (2008) describes a new and distinct journalistic role: the professional who always 'jumps in', is always available when the editor calls, and accepts assignments under all conditions. Hayes and Silke (2018, p. 1025) explain how digital labour is applied to freelancers, stating that new technologies are key structures of freelancers' work processes and tools that influence journalistic outcomes.

Several former studies describe the two-sided nature of freelance life, in which freelancers find themselves caught between autonomy and professional freedom on the one hand and precarity, constraints, and uncertainty on the other. Cohen discusses the contrast between entrepreneurs with portfolio careers and the precarious employment, uncertainty, and insecurity they experience. Job satisfaction seems high among freelancers, as they experience professional autonomy and personal freedom (Edström and Ladendorf, 2012; Mathisen, 2016; Cohen, 2016). They value the freedom to control their own working hours, flexibility, and the possibility of working with stories based on ideas they develop themselves (Edström and Ladendorf, 2012). Many freelancers also specialize in specific themes and thus become a kind of beat reporter. Freelancing might also allow them to work with longer formats than fast-paced news reporting (Mathisen, 2016), and it might provide the time and space to produce investigative, critical, and exploratory journalism (Cohen, 2016). Thus, professional possibilities are vital motivations for choosing a freelancing lifestyle. Das (2007) found that Australian freelancers perceive themselves as highly professional – even more professional than regularly employed journalists – because they operate independently within the industry.

However, freelancers also experience precarity, uncertainty, vulnerability, and increased commercial pressure (Mathisen, 2016; Cohen, 2016; Gollmitzer, 2020). Freelancers experience time pressures, financial insecurity, and poor payment, and they often occupy vulnerable positions (Das, 2007; Ladendorf, 2012; Gollmitzer, 2014; Mathisen, 2016). Freelancers are also challenged by shrinking rates, exploitation, poor working conditions, casualization, and pursuit of copyrights (Cohen, 2016). McKercher (2014) discusses the concept of 'piecework', in which freelancers work faster to produce enough stories to make a living. The freedom that accompanies the freelance life might also be characterized as an illusion of freedom in which the feeling of freedom is stronger than the actual freedom (Edstrøm and Ladendorf, 2012; Gollmitzer, 2014; Mathisen, 2016).

Investigative journalism is perceived to lie at the core of the journalistic identity, and it is valued as an essential function of journalism in democracy. However, precarity increases concerns about the decline of investigative and critical reporting because freelancers are not compensated adequately for such work (Hayes and Silke, 2019). Researchers and practitioners have expressed concern about the possibility of freelancers engaging in resource-intensive investigative journalism (Walters et al., 2006; Gollmitzer, 2014; Cohen, 2016). Thus, external institutional structures and forces affecting media work also affect the journalistic content presented to the public, as well as the societal role of journalism.

Being a semi-profession, professional work ethics are vital to defining the borders of journalism (Raaum, 1999). Former studies have also shed light on the ethical aspects of freelancing (Edström and Ladendor, 2012; Obermaier and Koch, 2014; Mathisen, 2018). The possible solitude of freelancing might be challenging, in that freelancers must deal with difficult ethical dilemmas on their own without having the newsroom to rely on and colleagues with whom to discuss issues. However, many freelancers develop support strategies to solve ethical dilemmas and seek discretionary guidance (Mathisen, 2018, p. 9). They construct their own networks that support their professional and ethical values (Philips, 2012).

Freelancers might also experience the duality between professional ideals and commercial demands on a more personal level than employed journalists (Mathisen, 2018, p. 5), because the professional role as a journalist and the entrepreneurial role of being self-employed might collide (Ladendorf, 2012, p. 89). This also addresses which kind of assignments freelancers take – only journalistic work or also PR and information work? In general, journalists hold a highly negative perception of PR work (McNamara, 2016). However, many freelancers also take on other job assignments within the PR sector because they cannot make a living from journalism alone (Bittner, 2011). PR assignments might be attractive, with structured workdays and good money (Frölich et al., 2013, p. 812). Ladendorf (2012) finds that freelancers conduct themselves according to journalistic ideals; however, most of them also take assignments outside the borders of journalism. She finds that individual ethics might have replaced professional principles and that freelancers stretch their ethical boundaries to earn a living (p. 92). Taking assignments within PR and communications might also evoke inter-role conflicts because PR workers primarily serve particular clients' interests, while the professional ideal of journalism is to hold power to account (Obermaier and Koch, 2015, p. 618). Working with PR might conflict with the journalists' commitment to autonomy, independence, truth, and neutrality (Frölich et al., 2013, p. 810). Obermaier and Koch (2015) imply that inter-role conflicts negatively influence the professional identity of the freelance journalists concerned. They find that such conflicts are an unpleasant experience for the freelancers affected, and they feel more stressed at work and report lower job satisfaction. Gollmitzer (2021) discusses how casually employed journalists describe and re-define their professional integrity as they struggle with the consequences of precarity. Based on an interview study with Canadian and German journalists, she finds that they subsidize journalistic work with other jobs or assignments.

In her recent study of Swedish freelancers, Norbäck (2021) discusses how the neoliberal discourse has a performative effect. 'The neoliberal worker embodies the ethos of our era, as her market-driven work conditions are perceived as a positive source of empowerment, autonomy and agency' (p. 4). This entrepreneurial subjectivity is both a consequence of the current neoliberal paradigm of an economic order, and a prerequisite (Vallas and Christin, 2018; Norbäck, 2021, p. 13). A core issue in this volume is how the tension between disruption and resilience affects journalism as a profession – more specifically concentrated around boundary disputes – the tension between precarity and autonomy, and the shifting professional landscape with its internal cleavages (see Chapter 1 for a more thorough discussion). A significant disruption of media work is found in the rise of less permanent employment posts and an increasing number of professionals working outside the established newsrooms. In the internal hierarchy within the profession, freelancers have been acknowledged only scarcely for their professional prestige (Hovden, 2008). Thus, the freelancers' working conditions are of vital interest (Gollmitzer, 2014, p. 826), affecting both the practitioners' collective behaviour as well as the shaping and reshaping of the boundaries of journalism (Carlson and Lewis, 2015). A corporatist-democratic country such as Norway (Hallin and Mancini, 2009), where the Nordic model in work life constitutes a vital framework (Hvid and Falkum, 2019) and the safety nets of the welfare state are rather stable, is an interesting case. The sociology of professions, as elaborated in Chapter 2, is a well-suited frame to analyze through, with both autonomy and boundary work as essential concepts.

Methods

The chapter is based on a quantitative survey among Norwegian freelancers conducted in spring 2019. Respondents were recruited from three organizations: the freelance department of the Norwegian union for journalists, the Press Photographers Association, and the Norwegian Critics' Association. The survey was distributed by e-mail via Questback to 1,147 people; 483 responses were received which gave a response rate of 42 percent. Respondents who turned out to be pensioners or in a regularly employed position were not included, leaving a total of 420 respondents. The questionnaire was transferred into the statistical program SPSS for analysis.

The sample is based on organization membership. The sampling method might be questioned, as it excludes freelancers without union membership. Consequently, the important experiences of freelancers outside the professional community might be overlooked. Young freelancers and atypical workers, especially in new online media, have a weaker tendency to organize (Deuze and Fortunati, 2011). However, despite these omissions, the sampling method was chosen for practical reasons since there are no other kinds of registers or overviews of freelancers.

Internet-based surveys tend to have a lower response rate than more direct and outreaching methods, such as phone surveys or personal interviews. A response rate of 42 percent might be perceived as relatively high. Given the strategic sampling method, we might characterize the rate as relatively satisfying. The survey consisted of 78 questions, all closed with predefined categories. The survey was distributed twice, and the majority of the responses were received quite promptly after the first round. The questionnaire touched upon issues such as working conditions, income and finance, job motivation, job satisfaction, relation to the assigners, ethical dilemmas, and health. Some of the questions could be problematic, as we asked respondents to recapture income and experiences in retrospect. As the survey was limited to freelancers, we could not compare their experiences with assigners' descriptions of how freelancers were allocated assignments.

The questionnaire was designed in cooperation with the aforementioned union and associations, which also actively encouraged their members to reply. Indeed the study's initiation originally came from the unions in cooperation with the Fritt Ord Foundation, as these called for more research-based knowledge about the working conditions for freelancers. The Fritt Ord Foundation supported the study financially, while the unions' role was limited to contributing to what questions were to be addressed as well as informing their members about the survey and encouraging participation. Even if the unions were given an active role in this part of the process, we must underline that as researchers, we made the final decisions related to the survey and are responsible for the analysis and interpretation.

A limitation of a quantitative survey is that we miss the opportunity to ask follow-up questions and go in depth, and the respondents cannot fill out or provide nuances with their own descriptions. Predefined categories do not always suit all respondents. On the other hand, the method ensures a large pool of quantitative data that are well suited to give broad and more conclusive findings regarding vital patterns and characteristics of the topic. As former studies of Norwegian freelancers are mainly qualitative, a quantitative survey entails a vital contribution to the existing knowledge.

Finally, we also must underline that the study was carried out one year before the COVID-19 epidemic stuck the world. The epidemic hit freelancers hard, as many of them lost assignments and contracts from one day to another when social distancing was practiced and travelling restricted. In Norway, the state financed a range of economic supports; however, these arrangements did not benefit all freelancers. Thus, the working conditions we describe in this chapter might have changed or even deteriorated since the research was conducted.

Description of the sample

Before diving into the analysis, we offer a brief description of the sample and explain some background variables to provide a picture of the response group.

Regarding sex, the number of male and female respondents was fairly equal, as 52 percent of our respondents were female, and 48 percent male. By contrast, 43 percent of the members of the Norwegian Union of Journalists are female. Regarding age, the substantial number of respondents was between 41 and 50 years of age. More than half of the respondents were 41 years old or above, while less than ten percent of the respondents were between 20 to 30 years old. These findings contradict earlier studies, as younger journalists are more often obliged to work as freelancers when entering the field (Walters et al., 2006). Several factors might have caused the low number of young respondents in our study. One explanation might be that young freelancers do not bother to participate in surveys such as this one. Another might be that young freelancers are less likely to have a union membership and therefore were excluded by our sampling method (see Deuze, 2011).

Eighty percent of the sample was educated at a higher level and held a three-year bachelor's degree from a university or university college, at a minimum. Thirty-five percent held a master's degree, more so females than males: 43 percent of females, 27 percent of males. Four percent had a PhD degree, and here the share between men and women was equal. Thus, the educational level among freelance journalists seems to be high, especially among female freelancers. Many precarious workers today are well

Table 4.1 Overview of the sample regarding age, sex, and level of education. (percent)

Age	Total	Male	Female	N
20–30	11	10	12	45
31–40	25	21	28	103
41–50	29	29	29	120
51–60	24	27	22	102
61 or over	12	14	10	50
Level of education				
High school	11	17	5	46
Bachelor's degree	35	35	34	145
Master's degree	35	27	43	148
PhD	4	4	3	15
Other	16	17	15	66
N=	420	203	217	

educated but experience uncertain career progression and a poor pay rate (Standing, 2011). Forty-two percent of the participants had previously been regularly employed in a media company prior to becoming freelancers. We will return to the reasons why respondents changed to freelance work later in the text.

The physical workplace constitutes an essential framework for daily professional practice. The vast majority of our respondents worked alone. Half of them (56 percent) worked from their home office, four percent worked by themselves from a rented office, whilst 40 percent worked in different varieties of professional collectives. Many of the respondents worked for a variety of different assigners: half of them claimed to work for two to five assigners in the year prior to the survey, while 20 percent had ten assigners or more. By contrast, two percent responded they had no assigners at all, and nine percent worked solely for a single assigner. As the previously discussed definition of freelancers requires working for several assigners, one could of course question whether these can be defined as freelancers at all, or if they were placed in an arrangement where they actually should be categorized as temporarily employed. However, it can also be a result of the difficulties of accessing enough assignments to make freelancing a viable or reasonable living.

When elaborating on the findings, we first describe the content of freelance work as the freelancers reported it, before a more thorough exploration of autonomy on the one side, and precarious conditions on the other. This is followed by a closer elaboration of those who considered leaving the media business altogether.

Content of work

We mapped what journalistic genres the freelancers mostly worked with and found an overall tendency that the longer formats dominate, such as documentaries and feature stories (46 percent). Also opinion journalism was vital (24 percent culture review, 2 percent columns), while 16 percent worked mostly with news and 12 percent with other genres. Consequently, it seems as if daily news coverage is not the freelancers' arena. Thirty-five percent stated they were primarily beat reporters with specialized fields, 27 percent were all-rounders, while the remaining 38 percent stated a combination of all-round reporting from a variety of issues and fields, and some specialized beats. From this we might draw a pattern where niches and beat reporting is a vital characteristic of freelance work, mostly communicated through genres offering depth and longer formats, which former studies also support (Mathisen, 2016).

We asked respondents whether they had carried out investigative and/or data-driven journalism in the three months prior to the survey. Twenty-one percent reported that they had, 66 percent said no, and 13 percent answered that this was 'not relevant' for them. Here, we might underline that we haven't analyzed the journalistic output freelancers produced; the amount of investigative journalism is based on how the freelancers reported their own work. Further, we asked whether they combined journalistic work with PR/ communications work. Thirty-nine percent stated they did, 61 percent stated no. In other words, a substantially larger amount of freelance work is carried out in the blurred zones rather than work considered to be professional or 'pure' work such as investigative journalism. Several scholars have problematized the scarce possibilities for freelancers to do investigative journalism because it doesn't pay well (Cohen, 2016; Hayes and Silke, 2018). Our study substantiates this fear, as nearly twice as many freelancers accepted assignments outside the borders of journalism than those undertaking investigative reporting. Since investigative reporting is perceived to be the core of professional journalistic activity, one might also assume that freelancers working with investigative reporting also enjoy the highest professional status among freelancers. On the other hand, working with PR might conflict with the professional ideals of journalism, thus impacting negatively on professional identity (Frölich et al., 2013) and challenging the boundaries of journalism (Bjerke et al., 2019). Freelancers also develop their own, individual boundary settings (Ladendorf, 2012). They develop different coping strategies, where communication work for museums, churches, and non-profit organizations are compatible with journalistic integrity, while communication work for corporations and content marketing is not (Gollmitzer, 2021).

However, the division lines are not as clear as might be expected. When crossing those who work with investigative reporting with those taking assignments within PR, we found that 43 percent of freelancers who had been working with investigative reporting had also been taking assignments within PR and communications work. In total, nine percent of the sample did both. This nuances the perception of demarcation lines within freelance journalism. The divisions between those who are perceived to work with free and sober journalism and those in the more questionable parts of work are more blurred and complicated than might be expected. For nearly ten percent of our sample, it was not a question of either/or. They conducted investigative reporting while accepting commercial assignments, which must be taken into consideration when discussing freelancers' professional identity.

A limitation of a quantitative survey is that we could not ask how the freelancers perceived this combination, and our questionnaire did not supply data to elaborate inter-role conflicts (Frölich et al., 2013). However, qualitative studies have shown how freelancers express ambivalence concerning commercial assignments, yet still consider these assignments necessary to finance the real and pure journalism. Some freelancers even use the concept of 'money jobs' to describe the commercial assignments, contrasting with the real journalism (Mathisen, 2018; Gollmitzer, 2021). As such, we can assume that at least some of the freelancers accept commercial assignments to finance more time- and resource-demanding investigative reporting, also as a strategy to justify their assignments within the blurred zones. This can moreover be interpreted as an expression of the balance between commerce and ideals within journalism on a very personal level, with which the single freelancers have to cope.

Entrepreneurial autonomy

To further elaborate the tensions between autonomy and precarity that define freelance life according to a range of former studies, we aimed to explore several aspects concerning autonomy, job satisfaction, and empowerment. First, the motivation for being a freelancer.

Figure 4.1 shows approximately a half and half split between 'volunteers and conscripts': 47 percent actively chose to freelance. The rest became freelancers due to different reasons that might be characterized as forced or 'having little choice'; 11 percent reported they aspired for permanent employment but failed to get a post. Nine percent experienced downsizing and lost their former permanent job, while 26 percent reported there were no permanent positions available within their fields. There are few permanent positions available for cultural review in Norwegian media companies. We also found that the grade of voluntariness increased with age: only 24

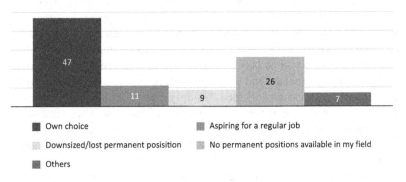

■ Own choice   ■ Aspiring for a regular job

■ Downsized/lost permanent posisition   ■ No permanent positions available in my field

■ Others

Figure 4.1 Why did you become a freelancer? (percent)

percent of the freelancers between 20 and 30 years old report that freelance life was a result of their own active choice. The share of voluntariness is highest in the ages between 51–60, where 55 percent had chosen to work as freelancers. It seems as though age and experience are vital factors in explaining whether journalists actively seek freelance life and might indicate that when young professionals are freelancers, they have few (if any) options because of a lack of any regular employment. This might also indicate that professional experience makes it easier to master freelance life. We also found a slightly higher degree of voluntariness among the freelancers working in investigative journalism compared to those combining this with PR work: 53 percent versus 48 percent. Norbäck (2021, p. 7) finds the same duality between freelancers choosing this mode, and freelancers forced into it by a lack of viable options.

We also asked respondents that actually chose a freelance lifestyle about their motivation for doing so. Fifty-seven percent reported professional freedom and possibilities as their most important motivation. Next, the possibility to use their special competence or act as beat reporters within specialized fields (18 percent) was cited. Thus, professional motivation seems to be the most important reason for choosing freelancing. We also found that freelancers working with investigative journalism reported special competence/ beat reporting as important to a higher degree than the rest of the sample: 23 percent stated this as their most important motivation. It seems as though specialized knowledge and competence might ease the possibilities to go in depth and work in investigative journalism.

Autonomy is a building block in professional ideology (Deuze, 2008). We asked about the origin of the stories they worked on: whether it was the freelancers who created their own ideas or whether it was the editors who assigned specific cases or stories. Seventy percent reported they either mostly worked with their own ideas, or that it was approximately half. These answers give a reason to conclude that professional autonomy might be a vital aspect of freelancing. Freelancers experience opportunities to follow their own ideas and define what types of stories and cases to work on, and this might contrast at least in some ways to regularly employed journalistic work: in hasty, downsized newsrooms with high production demands, the working conditions for news journalists are described as akin to running around in a hamster wheel, rewriting and re-packaging others' stories, which leaves scarce possibilities to work in depth or develop their own ideas and stories (Nygren, 2008; Lee- Wright et al., 2012). When we also consider that the majority of freelancers have specialized competencies within a certain field, or combine this with all-round reporting, we find several strong indications that professional autonomy in many ways is a distinct perceived advantage of freelance life. As such, our survey supports the findings of several former qualitative studies that have explored freelancers' perceptions through deeper descriptions. Freelancers highlight their professional autonomy and experience that many profession-advancing possibilities come along with freelance life (Massey and Elmore, 2011; Edstrøm and Ladendorf, 2012; Gollmitzer, 2014; Mathisen, 2016; Cohen, 2016).

Several of these former studies also conclude that job satisfaction among freelancers is high. The same pattern was found in our study.

As Figure 4.2 shows, in total, 75 percent described their motivation to be good or very good, while only 7 percent describe it as awful or bad. Seventeen percent responded, 'Okay, but nothing more than that'. Thus, job satisfaction seems to be overwhelmingly good.

To further elaborate on how job satisfaction develops over time, we also asked about their current job satisfaction compared to the previous three years. Job satisfaction was mainly unchanged, with 44 percent reporting no difference. Twenty-one percent reported a negative development, and 21 percent reported a positive development. We also discovered that whether freelancers undertook investigative reporting or combined journalism and PR work, this did not have any significant impact on job satisfaction. In both cases, job satisfaction was generally high. However, it is worth noting that more than 20 percent reported negative development and experienced lower job satisfaction. A limitation with the study is that in the questionnaire, we did not ask *why* job satisfaction increased or decreased. However, it is reasonable to connect this negative development to poor working conditions and more demanding times. This leads us to the precarious aspects of freelancers' working conditions.

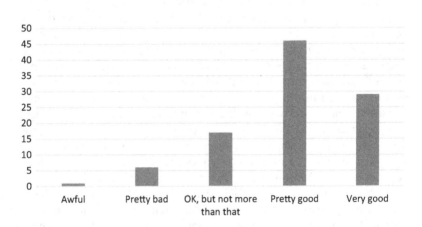

Figure 4.2 Job satisfaction among freelancers. (percent)

Precarious freelancers always at work

Wages and income are vital aspects of working conditions. In the survey, we asked several questions about economy and income. One significant finding is that the majority of the respondents worked part time as freelancers. Only 35 percent of the sample made a living from freelancing alone. A limitation of a quantitative survey is not having the possibility to ask follow-up questions, and thus we cannot conclude about the reasons for part-time work. However, former studies have suggested that freelancers work part time because they do not earn enough from freelancing alone (Bittner, 2011; Hayes and Silke, 2018; Gollmitzer, 2020). As discussed earlier in the chapter, two percent of the freelancers stated they did not have any assigners, while nine percent only had one. A lack of available assigners might cause part-time work. In addition, some of them combined journalism and PR work, as 38 percent of the respondents did.

When discussing working conditions, wages and income constitute one of the most basic concerns.

Figure 4.3 illustrates the income for full-time freelancers. Here, it is important to underline that this is the income level for those 35 percent living off of freelancing alone (stated in Norwegian kroner [NOK]). In contrast, industry wages for journalists average 620,671 NOK. A good deal of nuance is lost in such average wages, where type of publication, seniority, and position impact on personal wages for each journalist. Still, we found that only 22 percent of the freelancers earned more than the average wage for journalists, and 21 percent earned as little as 250,000 NOK, which is below the Norwegian poverty measure. We also must remember that the sample in general is highly educated, as previously discussed. One conclusion we can draw from this is that the financial differences between freelancers are huge. Some freelancers seem to enjoy a rather robust and resilient freelance life, earning good money, while freelancers on the other end of

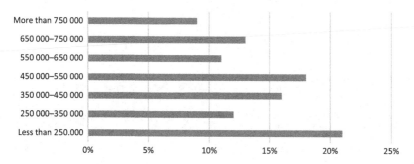

Figure 4.3 Income for full time freelancers in NOK. (percent)

the scale struggle. Wages are significantly low, and the majority struggle to earn enough to support themselves and a family. It even seems that wages have worsened over the years. Nineteen percent, or every fifth freelancer, reported that they were paid less per job than they were three years ago, while 41 percent stated they earned exactly the same, despite a general rise in price and wages. The same deterioration of wages for some freelancers is present in former studies (Cohen, 2016; Deuze and Witschge, 2018). In Sweden, 60 percent of freelance journalists earn less than the collective agreement's lowest rate for journalist employment (Norbäck, 2021, p. 2).

In terms of income and wages, precarity is a distinct characteristic of freelance life, with low wages and even declining income characterizing a vast amount of freelancers and also underlining the precariousness for highly educated professionals (Standing, 2011). Given that the majority work part time as journalists, freelancing seems a risky and uncertain business when material conditions decline. Considering the majority of freelancers are paid below the average industry wage may contribute to the polarization and increased professional cleavages regarding status, which also might weaken the collective professional identity. As Cohen (2016, p. 111) states:

> Freelance writing is highly individualized, which makes it difficult to address labour–capital power relations. (…) The organization of freelance work prevents writers from recognizing that they face common challenges linked to structural conditions.

The precarious aspect of freelancing worsens when we asked about how they controlled time, as elaborated in the figure below.

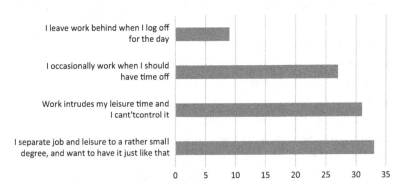

Figure 4.4 Description of work-leisure balance. (percent)

Here, the respondents were asked to mark the statement that described their situation the best. We saw that nine percent, less than one in ten freelancers, left work behind when they log off for the working day. Twenty-seven percent did occasionally work even if they had planned to take time off, such as at evenings and weekends, while 31 percent perceived that work intruded into their leisure time, in a manner and to an extent beyond their control. In contrast, 33 percent divided life between job and free time to a limited degree, wanted to have it as such, and were satisfied with the situation. As several studies have shown, freelancers value the flexibility and possibility to control and manage their own working hours (Das, 2007; Edström and Ladendorf, 2012; Mathisen, 2016), which we also define in this study. For some, this flexibility is a lifestyle and the core of freelance life, even the main reason to avoid regular employment. Still, a third of the sample felt that they did not control their work time and that they had to work in the evenings and on weekends. If we also add the bad financial conditions discussed above, the precarious and vulnerable aspects of freelancing are forcefully underlined. The precarity entails short planning horizons, fluctuating levels of work, and uncertainty about future jobs (Norbäck, 2021, p. 7). Still, it is worth noting that difficulties with separating work and leisure is a vital characteristic of all entrepreneurial work, free and creative crafts of every kind, as well as journalistic work in general. Also regularly employed journalists report the same tension between work and leisure (Grimsmo and Heen, 2013).

The difficulty of managing time was also expressed when we investigated whether the respondents felt forced to accept tasks they actually did not have time to complete, in fear of losing future assignments.

Table 4.2 shows that a total of 63 percent of all respondents had accepted work, even if they really had no available working time to complete it, forcing them to work long hours and contributing to the perception of the lack of work-leisure balance discussed above. Of course, freelance work might not always be predictable, and most freelancers probably will experience busy periods as well as periods with less work. Even if a freelancer's schedule

Table 4.2 Have you accepted assignments you did not really have time for, in fear of losing assignments in the future? (percent)

	All	Freelancers working in investigative journalism	Freelancers combining with PR and communication
Yes	63	64	74
No	37	36	26
N=	420	88	163
Correlation		.026	.191

is full, it might be difficult to decline work if an editor calls because being available is a vital asset for freelancers. Similarly, in her study, Norbäck (2021, p. 9) finds that freelancers are reluctant to turn down assignments. Referrals and previous jobs are mechanisms that can create the next job. Freelances fear that declining a job could reduce the possibility for future assignments, a situation Nygren (2008) describes as the professional who always jumps in, no matter what time and conditions.

Table 4.2 also shows a tendency that freelancers working with PR and communications experience this more often than both the sample as a whole and freelancers working within investigative journalism. The difference is as high as ten percent and supports the notion that freelancers combining journalism and PR often do so out of need. Ideally, they want to limit their work to pure journalistic assignments; however, when the supply of assignments is restricted and payment is bad, some freelancers choose to accept jobs outside the border of journalism to be able to meet their outgoings (Mathisen, 2018).

Uncertain future

As discussed above, freelance life is characterized by a paradoxical and self-contradicting tension between highly valued professional autonomy and job satisfaction on the one hand, and a number of precarious working conditions on the other. The work-leisure balance is difficult to maintain, where payments are getting worse and it is difficult to make a living by freelancing alone. In our study, we also discovered that 39 percent combined journalism with PR and communication work, which also encompasses inter-role conflicts. Thus, autonomy and freedom seem to be more perceived and idealized than approximating the realities of freelance life.

Given these increasingly precarious conditions, what are their future plans? Do freelancers see a future within journalism or do they plan to change their careers? We asked whether the respondents considered leaving journalism or the media business.

Table 4.3 reveals that 26 percent answered yes, 50 percent no, while 24 percent were unsure. There is also a tendency for freelancers working in investigative journalism to be less likely to leave, while those combining PR and communication work were more eager to leave. From this, we might assume that the available nature of work does matter: working with investigative journalism increases the likelihood of staying within the profession. Combining journalism and PR work might be perceived as less professionally satisfying, as the tendency to leave increases and the willingness to stay decreases. However, as discussed earlier, we found no difference in job satisfaction between these two categories of freelancers, which

Table 4.3 Would you consider leaving the media business? (percent)

	All	Freelancers working in investigative journalism	Freelancers combining with PR and communication
Yes	26	20	30
No	50	53	44
Unsure	24	25	25
N=	420	88	163
Correlation		.026	.037

nuances the perception of combining journalism and PR work as being less satisfying.

Even if half the freelancers did not have plans to leave media work and the freelance life, the other half did, or were unsure whether they would. This makes it vital to elaborate more on how those who consider leaving the business perceive their working conditions. Obviously, access to assignments is important. Forty-seven percent of freelancers who considered leaving the media business reported that it was difficult to gain enough assignments to make a living. Seventy percent had accepted assignments they really did not have enough time for, in fear of losing future jobs. Forty-five percent expressed that work intruded into their leisure time and that the balance between being on and off the job was difficult to handle. Thus, it seems as though poor working conditions emerge as a main reason why some freelancers consider leaving the business completely. Another distinct characteristic is that a large amount of the freelancers who considered breaking out of the field were more or less forced into freelancing; less than 30 percent had chosen freelance life themselves. For comparison, in the sample as a whole, 47 percent had actively chosen freelance life.

In comparison, in her study of German and Canadian freelancers, Gollmitzer (2021) finds that none of the freelancers with long experience in journalism had decided to leave, despite the precarious working conditions; however, many voiced it as a possibility if working conditions deteriorated further. 'What keeps many of them from leaving journalism is their enjoyment in work based on types and degrees of autonomy and independence rarely found in other types of work', she states (p. 9). Still, the fact that a quarter of the freelancers in our study considered leaving journalism may cause concern regarding future recruitment of journalists and the stability of the profession. The number of journalists in the profession has significantly reduced in the past decades. If a quarter of the freelance corps do realize their intended ambitions to leave the business, the profession would utterly decline. However, this might also be interpreted as a significant description of the fragility and demanding nature of the working conditions that freelancers confront. Despite high job satisfaction and professional autonomy, the precariousness is challenging in a way that pushes some of them out of the media business, especially for those combining journalistic assignments with work outside the borders of journalism.

Concluding discussion

In this chapter, we have addressed and hopefully answered the research question: *what characterizes the working conditions of freelance journalists in the tension between precarity and autonomy?* We found a distinct and overwhelming high job satisfaction, combined with a perception of high professional autonomy, which also emerged as the most important motivation to choose freelance life. In many ways, this is compatible with a description of journalism as a mission or lifestyle (see Chapter 2) where a range of individual and professional possibilities can be realized. The majority also reported that job satisfaction was unchanged across the last three years. These findings contrast sharply with several precarious working conditions, where the wages are low (and have even decreased in recent years), working hours are difficult to control, and freelancers dare not decline assignments they do not have time to take on. In other words, the perception of the flexible, free, and autonomous freelance life is paradoxically contrasted by a picture of freelancers always available and always at work, while receiving markedly lower remuneration than their employed colleagues.

Journalism constitutes a societal institution as well as a professional field. The distinctly precarious working conditions also demonstrate how the structural framework outside the profession affects the working conditions and professional possibilities inside. The neoliberal turn brings a more precarious and fragile media work life. Even within the framework of the Nordic model of work life with its welfare safety nets, the work life for highly educated freelance journalists remains precarious, fragile, unstable, and offers poor working conditions. This leads to a more uncertain future since a quarter of the freelancers in our study had considered leaving journalism. Not surprisingly, we found that those who considered leaving experienced the most precarious working conditions. Thus, it seems that bad working conditions might push freelancers out of a job they value for its autonomy and professional possibilities. Within a profession already shrinking in numbers, a vital aspect to discuss is what impact this would have on the journalism profession if those freelancers actually left.

Still, a minority of the sample made good money and managed to control time. The description of freelance life within the Nordic model also contains a history of huge internal differences within the freelance field. One internal cleavage runs between those who actively want to be freelancers and those who are more or less forced into it. Another internal cleavage could be drawn between freelancers working within investigative journalism, which is at the core of professional practice and the kind of job that enjoys the highest professional value and prestige, and those in the blurred zones who also take assignments outside the borders of journalism.

The professionalization of journalism is a process where ideology continuously defines and re-defines what is considered as real journalism and who is regarded as a real journalist (Zelizer, 2004). One of the key struggles for journalistic autonomy has been the demarcation between journalism on the one side, and PR and communication work on the other (Carlson and Lewis, 2015), constituting the boundaries of journalism. However, we found that among the freelancers in our study, this distinction was not as clear as one could expect. Nine percent of our sample were doing both, and 43 percent of the freelancers working within investigative journalism had also taken PR assignments. Thus, the demarcation line between what is regarded 'professional pure' and 'professional blurred' is complex to draw. Further, former qualitative studies find that freelancers combining journalism with PR argue with the necessity, as these assignments are better paid and finance the 'real and pure' journalism. Thus, this might be seen as an adaption strategy, which eventually can move the borders of journalism and affect the professional identity.

Several former studies have described the paradoxical tension between precarity and autonomy; many of them based on qualitative interview studies. Our quantitative survey confirms this double-edged nature as a distinct pattern of freelance life, which might affect how the demarcation line is drawn and thus the boundary struggles within the profession. The precarious employment conditions may contribute to a de-institutionalization, where the profession shrinks, the professional norms and values lose terrain, and the demarcation lines are at stake. However, the high autonomy and job satisfaction also bring hope and might contribute to strengthen the professional identity.

Our study provides some answers and raises new questions. The media landscape experiences rapid changes, as new media pave their way, contributing changed professional routines and work processes for journalists including freelancers. Essential aspects for further studies are how new media affect freelance work. For example, how do freelancers use social media in their work? Also, not to forget perhaps the most critical juncture of them all: how COVID-19 changed working life. For future studies of freelance life, it is mandatory to explore how the epidemic affected the professional life of freelancers.

References

Bittner, A.K. (2011) *Managing Change. Innovation and Trade Unionism in the News Industry*. Brussel: The European Federation of Journalists.

Bjerke, P., Fonn, B.K. and Mathisen, B.R. (eds.) (2019) *Journalistikk: profesjon i endring*. Stamsund: Orkana Akademisk [Journalism – a profession in change].

Carlson, M. and Lewis, S. (eds.) (2015) *Boundaries of Journalism. Professionalism, Practices and Participation*. London and New York: Routledge.

Cohen, N.S. (2016) *Writers' Rights: Freelance Journalism in a Digital Age*. Montreal & Kingston: McGill-Queen's University Press.

Cohen, N.S., Hunter, A. and O'Donnell, P. (2019) Bearing the burden of corporate restructuring: Job loss and precarious employment in Canadian journalism. In *Journalism Practice*, 13(7), pp. 817–833. DOI: 10.1080/17512786.2019.1571937

Das, J. (2007) Sydney freelance journalists and the notion of professionalism. In *Pacific Journalism Review*, 13 (1), pp. 142–160. Auckland, Australia. DOI: https://doi.org/10.24135/pjr.v13i1.890

Deuze, M. (2008) What is journalism? Professional identity and ideology of journalists reconsidered. *Journalism*, 6(4), pp. 442–464. London. Sage Publications. DOI: 10.1177/1464884905056815

Deuze, M. and Fortunati, L. (2011) *Atypical Newswork, Atypical Media Management, in Deuze, Mark. 2011. Managing Media Work*. London: Sage.

Deuze, M. and Witschge, T. (2018) Beyond journalism: Theorizing the transformation of journalism. *Journalism*, 19(2), pp. 165–181. DOI: 10.1177/1464884916688550

Edström, M. and Ladendorf, M. (2012) Freelance journalists as a flexible workforce in media industries. *Journalism Practice*, 6(5–6), pp. 711–721. DOI: 10.1080/17512786.2012.667275

Frölich, R., Koch, T. and Obermaier, M. (2013) What's the harm in moonlighting? A qualitative survey on the role conflicts of freelance journalists with secondary employment in the field of PR. *Media, Culture & Society*, 35(7), pp. 809–829. DOI: 10.1177/0163443713495076

Giddens, A. (2007) *Europe in the Global Age*. Cambridge: Polity Press.

Grimsmo, A. and Heen, H. (2013) *Journalistundersøkelsen 2013. Rapport fra Arbeidsforskningsinstituttet*. Oslo: Arbeidsforskningsinstituttet. [The journalist study].

Gollmitzer, M. (2014) Precariously employed watchdogs? *Journalism Practice*, 8(6), pp. 826–841. DOI: 10.1080/17512786.2014.882061

Gollmitzer, M. (2020) Employment conditions in Journalism. *Oxford Research Encyclopedia of Communication*, Oxford: Oxford University Press. pp. 1–28. https://doi.org/10.1093/acrefore/9780190228613.013.805

Gollmitzer, M. (2021) Journalism ethics with Foucault: Casually employed journalists' constructions of professional integrity. *Journalism*, pp. 1–19. DOI: 10.1177/14648849211036301

Hallin, D.C and Mancini, P. (2009) *Comparing Media Systems: Three Models of Media and Politics*. Cambridge: Cambridge University Press.

Hayes, K. and Silke H. (2018) The networked freelancer? Digital labour and freelance journalism in the age of social media. *Digital Journalism*, 6(8), pp. 1018–1028. DOI: 10.1080/21670811.2018.150538

Hayes, K. and Silke H. (2019) Narrowing the discourse? Growing precarity in freelance journalism and its effect on the construction of news discourse. In *Critical Discourse Studies*, 16(3), pp. 363–379. DOI: 10.1080/17405904.2019. 1570290.

Hovden, J.F. (2008) *Profane and sacred: A study of the Norwegian journalistic field.* Phd-dissertation. Bergen; University of Bergen.

Hunter, A. (2016) It's like having a second full-time job: Crowdfunding, journalism and labour. *Journalism Practice*, 10(2), pp. 217–232. DOI: 10.1080/17512786.2015.1123107

Hvid, H. and Falkum E. (eds.) (2019) *Work and Wellbeing in the Nordic Countries. Critical Perspectives on the World's Best Working Lives.* London and New York. Routledge.

Kalleberg, A.L. (2018) *Precarious Lives. Job Insecurity and Well-being in Rich Democracies.* Cambridgde: Polity Press.

Ladendorf, M. (2012) Freelance journalists' ethical boundary settings in information work. In *Nordicom Review*, 33(1), pp. 83–98. DOI: 10.2478/nor-2013-0006

Lee-Wright, P., Philips, A. and Witschge, T. (2012) *Changing Journalism.* London and New York. Routledge.

MacNamara J. (2016) The continuing convergence of journalism and PR: New insights for ethical practice from a three-country study of senior practitioners. In *Journalism and Mass Communication Quarterly*, 93(1), pp. 118–141. DOI: 10.1177/10776990`15605803

Mathisen, B.R. (2016) Entrepreneurs and idealists: Freelance journalists at the intersection of autonomy and constraints. In *Journalism Practice.* DOI: 10.1080/17512786.2016.1199284.

Mathisen, B.R. (2018) Ethical boundaries among freelance journalists. *Journalism Practice*, 13(6), pp. 639–656. DOI: 10.1080/17512786.2018.1548301

Marin-Sanchiz, C.R., Carvajal, M. and Gonzales-Esteban, J.L. (2021) Survival strategies in freelance journalism: An empowering toolkit to improve professionals' working conditions. *Journalism Practice*, pp. 1–24. DOI: 10.1080/17512786.2021.1929414

Massey, B.L. and Elmore, C.J. (2011) Happier working for themselves? *Journalism Practice*, 5(6), pp. 672–686. DOI: 10.1080/17512786.2011.579780

Massey, B.L. and Elmore, C.J. (2018) Freelancing in journalism. In Örnebring, H. and Wasserman, H. (eds.) *Oxford Research Encyclopedia of Communication.* Oxford, UK: Oxford University Press. https://doi.org/10.1093/acrefore /9780190228613.013.818

McKercher, C (2014) Precarious times, precarious work: A feminist political economy of freelance journalists in Canada and the United States. In Fuchs C. and Sandoval M. (eds.) *Critique, Social Media and the Information Society.* New York: Routledge, pp. 219–230.

Norbäck, M. (2021) Back to the future of journalist work? Entrepreneurial subjectivity and freelance journalism in Sweden. *Journalism*, pp 1–18. DOI:10.1177/14648849211033131

Nygren, G. (2008) *Yrke på glid: om journalistrollens de-professionalisering. (Profession on the slide – de- profesionalization of the journalistic role).* Stockholm: SIMO.

Obermaier, M. and Koch, T. (2015) Mind the gap: Consequences of inter-role conflicts of freelance journalists with secondary employment in the field of public relations. *Journalism*, 16(5), pp. 615–629. DOI: 10.1177/1464884914528142

O'Donnell, P., Zion, L. and Sherwood, M. (2016) Where do journalists go after newsroom job cuts? *Journalism Practice*, 10(1), pp. 35–51. DOI: 10.1080/17512786.2015.1017400

Örnebring, H. and Conill, R.F. (2016) Outsourcing newswork. In Witschge, T., Anderson, C.W., Domingo, D. and Hermida, A. (eds.) *The SAGE Handbook of Digital Journalism*. London: Sage, pp. 207–221.

Philips, A. (2012) Transparency and the ethics of new journalism. In Lee-Wright, P., Philips, A. and Witschge, T. (2012) *Changing Journalism*. London and New York: Routledge, pp. 135–144.

Raaum, O. (1999) *Pressen er løs! Fronter i journalistenes faglige frigjøring*. Oslo: Pax Forlag. [The press is loose. Fronts in journalists professional liberation]

Sennett, R. (2008) *The Craftsman*. New Haven. Yale University Press.

Standing, G. (2011) *The Precariat. The New Dangerous Class*. London. Bloomsbury Academic.

Vallas, S.P. and Christin, A. (2018) Work and identity in an era for precarious employment: How workers respond to 'personal branding' discourse. *Work and Occupations*, 45(1), pp. 3–37. DOI: 10.1177/0730888417735662

Van Leuven, S., Vanhaelewyn, B. and Raeymaeckers, K. (2021) From one division of labor to the other: The relation between beat reporting, freelancing, and journalistic autonomy. *Journalism Practice*, 15(9), pp. 1203–1221. DOI: 10.1080/17512786.2021.1910982

Wahl-Jorgensen, K. and Hanitzsch, T. (2009) *The Handbook of Journalism Studies*. New York: Routledge.

Walters, E., Warren, C. and Dobbie, M. (2006) *The Changing Nature of Work. A Global Survey and Case Study of Atypical Work in the Media Industry*. International Federation of Journalists. Switzerland: International Federation of Journalists.

Zelizer, B. (2004) *Taking Journalism Seriously: News and the Academy*. Thousand Oaks: Sage.

5 At the other end of precarity

Profiled columnists as branded goods

*Birgit Røe Mathisen and
Lisbeth Morlandstø*

Introduction

A significant trend in journalism in recent years has been the expansion of interpretative and commentary journalism in several countries (Salgado and Strömback, 2012; Esser and Umbrich, 2014; Fink and Schudson, 2014; Knapskog et al., 2016). This development implies that an increasing number of journalists work as columnists or commentators; their professional work involves interpreting, arguing, and expressing opinions concerning contemporary events and phenomena. This rise is an object of scholarly interest as well as political and public debate, with the growing power and influence of columnists as an essential concern. Profiled columnists are regarded as branded goods for their media companies. Digitization engenders development and innovation of the traditional commentary genre, as it is being transferred onto new formats and platforms, such as podcasts. These trends make it vital to shed light on columnists' professional roles and status. Several studies are concerned with commentary journalism as part of political communication, among others related to typical political scandals (Allern and Pollack, 2012). However, few studies focus on the columnist as a professional or occupational practitioner. Based on a series of interview studies with commentators across eight years, this chapter aims to fill this gap, asking the two-fold research question: *what characterizes the professional role of commentary journalists, and how does the genre's transformation into new formats affect this role?*

This volume focuses on changes in journalism; commentary journalism represents both change and stability. The stability is related to its strong historical roots, as interpretations and commentary are among the oldest forms of mediated discourse: commentary became an integral part of the press long before journalism as an institutional practice and profession was invented (Djerf-Pierre and Weibull, 2008, p. 211). The change is related to growth and expansion into new formats and whether the fragmented and digitized

DOI: 10.4324/9781003144724-5

media environment disrupts columnists' authority in public debate. On the following pages, we further elaborate both stability and change, tradition and history, as well as transformation, innovation, and challenges. The chapter addresses all three of the tensions elaborated in Chapter 1: between autonomy and precarity, boundary disputes and the internal cleavages in the profession. Before diving into the empirical data, we will briefly discuss the development as well as the characteristics of commentary journalism as they have been viewed in former research.

A growing genre

Commentary or opinion-based journalism is considered to be a specific genre within journalism, with its own norms and rules, a contract between the producer and the receiver, and where the receiver expects to meet views and interpretations. Political commentators are not expected to uphold the traditional journalistic norms of balance and neutrality as political reporters are; on the contrary, they are allowed and expected to give subjective interpretations and personal opinions. Salgado and Strömbäck (2012, p. 154) define interpretive journalism as opposed to descriptive, fact-focused, and source-driven journalism, characterized by a prominent journalistic voice and by journalistic explanations, evaluations, contextualizations, or speculations that go beyond verifiable facts or sources' statements. As we shall see, this definition also contains, but is not limited to, commentary journalism. The commentary genre is defined by its style and function, with the journalistic voice as a prominent element: the commentator is present in the text and wants to appear as an expert. The argumentative style might vary from an open, reflexive style to making clearer statements (Mathisen and Morlandstø, 2016). In any case, interpretative journalism emphasizes a strong journalistic voice, interpreting facts, and contextualizing events (Knapskog et al., 2016, p. 166).

The division between news and views is fundamental in journalism, with its roots reaching back to the early British newspaper in the 1600s. Nimmo and Combs even trace the origins of political punditry as far back as the philosophers of ancient Greece (Nimmo and Combs, 1992). In the Anglo American context, columnists originated in the US in the 1920s, with Walter Lippman an early and well-known practitioner (Duff, 2008; Bro, 2012). Later, both the party press and its dissolution were important for the development of commentary journalism. The party press offered a new type of political communication involving the use of subjective comments where journalists gained a new authority as interpreters of public discourse (Schudson, 1995). The dissolution of the party press also constituted a vital watershed creating a more independent and critical journalism. Further, the professionalization process within journalism, highlighting the critical role as the fourth estate, was essential for the development of commentary journalism (Mathisen and Morlandstø, 2016).

Fink and Schudson (2014) state that quantitatively the most significant change in newspaper journalism between the 1950s and the early 2000s is the rise of contextual reporting. Djerf-Pierre and Weibull (2008, p. 209) characterize the growth of interpretive journalism as one of the most significant changes in Swedish journalism over recent decades. Contextual and interpretive journalism contains more than simple overt and labelled commentaries and columns. However, the rise of commentary journalism is a significant part of these developments, and McNair (2008, p. 112) describes the growth of online opinion-based journalism as a 'commentary explosion'. In other words, significant change is related to growth and expansion.

Undoubtedly, newspapers both online and in print produce more commentaries and give more opinions than before (Knapskog et al., 2016, p. 172). Consequently, it might be assumed that the number of journalists working as commentators or columnists is increasing, even though a specific register of columnists is difficult to achieve. However, except for small local newsrooms, most media companies contain separate columnist departments employed by journalistic or political editors concerned with commentary work only. In scholarly literature, concepts such as *columnists*, *pundits*, and *commentators* are used. Bengtsson (2015) uses the concept of political commentator, which she defines as: 'a person who is framed by national broadcast or print media as a political insider and given the time or space to advance his or her personal political interpretations on a regular basis' (p. 7). Raabe (2018) defines commentators as 'the full-time editorial staff that are permanent contributors of opiniated and analytical political content to their respective newspapers' (p. 17). In this chapter, we use the words *commentators* and *columnists*.

Many past and contemporary political commentators were originally trained as and have worked as journalists, and they often depend on the work of other journalists (Bro, 2012, p. 435) – for example, news journalists and political reporters. Becoming a columnist is mostly a career path for experienced journalists and seldom the first way into journalism for newcomers in the field.

Societal role

Scholars mainly analyze the growth of commentary related to political communication and political commentary (Djerf-Pierre and Weibull, 2008; McNair, 2008; Allern, 2010; Rogstad, 2016; Raabe, 2018). Scholars also discuss *why* we see this characteristic expansion, with explanations given at different levels. One explanation is that decreasing trust in political institutions in most modern democracies has caused a greater need for critical journalism, with independent interpretations of politics (Nord et al., 2012). Another explanation is that a fragmented public sphere with information overload, where everyone might give their statements in blogs and social media, causes an increased need for qualified commentators to guide the audience, helping them sort out the overload of information fragments (Knapskog et al., 2016; Mathisen and Morlandstø, 2016, 2019). As Raabe (2018, p. 7) writes, the rise of online alt-right news outlets, the spread of fake news, the fragmentation of the public sphere, and the intensified information divide all increase the importance of high-quality commentary written by professionals with privileged access to political sources.

A third explanation is that when political communication, political spin, and PR become professionalized, a journalistic response is needed in the political discourse. Here, commentary journalism is seen as a form of counter-spin, where journalists fight back in the public sphere (McNair, 2000). Thus, opinionated journalism becomes an institutionalized counter-power in public. A fourth explanation involves media economy, where it is argued that commentary is a less expensive form of journalism compared to more resource-demanding investigative journalism and news reporting in the field (McNair, 2000). Political commentators help to fill the 24/7 news cycle, and Bro (2008, p. 197) argues that views-oriented journalism allows for fast and inexpensive production with political commentators as a popular source.

These explanations are rooted in professional theory as well as an institutional approach to journalism. The former is concerned with developing the professional role of columnists and how the line is drawn between professional columnists on the one hand and opinionated practices such as blogging and citizen participation on the other. In other words, valuing the societal need for the professional columnist could be interpreted as a boundary dispute (Gieryn, 1983; Carlson, 2015), underlining the fact that professional columnists guarantee a form of quality that bloggers and influencers do not. The lenses of professional theory also underline societal acknowledgment of the legitimacy of journalism. Playing an essential role in the public sphere and democracy, opinionated journalism composes a vital part of the institutional role of journalism, as it contributes to debate, enlightenment, controversy, and critique (Mathisen and Morlandstø, 2016). Columnists have a particular role in the social information chain, as their prime function is clarification (Duff, 2008, p. 232). Knapskog et al. (2016, p. 166) state that the core rationale for the journalistic institution lies in its capability for principled deliberation. Further, the institution is committed to providing interpretative frameworks that explain and identify causes and provide a forum where contending interpretations can be questioned and evaluated. Commentators are important bearers of the shared frames of reference in society, which are a crucial aspect of any democracy (Raabe, 2018, p. 19). As stated by Salgado and Strömbäck (2012, p. 156), there is a rather wide consensus that an important democratic function of journalism is to provide people with the kind of information they need to be free and self-governing.

However, in scholarly as well as political debate, a broad critique of the rising commentariat has been raised involving whether it displaces fact-based, investigative journalism and reporting from the field. An essential discussion is whether the commentators become too powerful, just reproducing the perspectives of the societal elites (Raabe, 2018, p. 9). Another critique is related to the fact that political columnists favour the political debate as a 'horse race' and do not contribute to an enlightened public debate – on the contrary, they contribute to a stupefying exchange of views (Lysbakken and Isaksen, 2008). Actors in society question the societal power of columnists as professionals, expressing a lack of trust and raising doubts about the legitimacy of commentary journalism (Bengtson, 2015). However, scholars also interpret the commentariat positively. The argumentative role of journalists to comment on or analyze political developments has been widely acknowledged as a basic professional function and a necessary complement to objective reporting (Nord et al., 2012, p. 88). Knapskog et al. (2016) argue that in times of fragmentation, the commentary genre might be one of the keys for professional journalism to renew its contract with an increasingly demanding and fragmented audience, constituting a powerful weapon to defend the professional autonomy of journalism and produce relevant knowledge and intellectual resources to cope with present challenges in journalism.

Genre innovation and branding

Genres are based on interaction between conventions and expectations (Lindgren, 2016). However, genres develop and change (Liestøl and Morrison, 2015). Social media increasingly impacts on the distribution of columns, and newsrooms experiment and attempt new commentary formats and new ways to communicate with their audiences (Mathisen and Morlandstø, 2018; Morlandstø and Mathisen, 2016, 2018). For instance, podcasts have paved the way for a more personalized and intimate journalism (Lindgren, 2016). Being involved in genre development and newsroom innovation also implies autonomy and creativity in work for the professionals involved. Newsrooms innovate, developing contextual and interpretive genres to sustain their societal role, and innovations are legitimized out of commercial as well as professional motives: to strengthen the institutional values of journalism and the newsroom as a brand (Mathisen and Morlandstø, 2018, p. 43).

In the socially stratified field of journalism, columnists are placed in the prestigious sphere of the profession (Hovden, 2008). Political commentators have always enjoyed a high level of status, influence, and fame (Raabe, 2018, p. 5). Columnists are often valued as the prized assets of media companies. News media have upgraded the market value of interpretation and opinion-making. As commentary journalism has emerged steadily as a more important genre, cultivation of a layer of celebrity columnists has increased (Rogstad, 2016). Such columnists are also called political pundits (Nimmo and Combs, 1992), or the 'political priesthood' (Raabe, 2018). Profiled commentators become important flagships for their media companies, building celebrity and profiling the individual commentators as important brands (Djerf-Pierre and Weibull, 2008; Rogstad, 2016; Raabe, 2018). Profiled and branded columnists create digital engagement and audience loyalty for the newsrooms. In competitive news markets, political commentators have transgressive potential in the way they can be used outside their own news organizations and moonlight as publicity agents (Bro, 2012, p. 442). For instance, when newspaper commentators are invited into the broadcast studios to comment on politics, they also contribute to the branding of the media company. Commentators are expected to build community, and make bonds with and secure loyalty from readers (Knapskog et al., 2016, p. 172). One might expect that there will be even more pressure for individualization in the future, which might tempt columnists to shout louder or go into more entertaining modes (Duff, 2008, p. 241). Social media also increases the potential for journalistic self-promotion (Olaussen, 2018). We also see that distinct opinions gain more traffic on social media through shares and likes, and thus contribute to the visibility of media companies as well as individual columnists (Mathisen and Morlandstø, 2018). Self-promotion might become more significant than news brands (Hedman, 2015; Usher, 2020). As Usher (2020) states, 'Celebrified columnists both create and are pseudo-events. They highlight and reframe news and act as central points for audiences to share experiences, which through them become mediated and mutual' (p. 5).

Data and methods

The authors of this chapter have studied commentary journalism and columnists in three different studies across a time span of eight years (2013–2021): each study has been conducted in the stratified Norwegian media context. The three studies constitute the empirical ground of this chapter. In our first project, carried out in 2013 and 2014, we interviewed 11 columnists and editors in six regional newsrooms. Additionally, we designed a content analysis and a qualitative argumentative analysis of columns. Our second project began in 2015 and was based on a case analysis of two innovative ventures developing new genre formats. We focused on commentary and explanatory journalism in two of the regional media sources from the former study, namely *Nordnorsk debatt* in the newspaper *Nordlys*, and *Brif* in the newspaper *Bergens Tidende*. Both represent genre innovation in digital formats. *Brif* was an innovation related to explanatory journalism on the web, and we interviewed six editors and journalists/columnists (four men and two women). *Nordnorsk debatt* represented an innovative online commentary platform devoted to opinion-based content, editorial columns, and audience contributions. In this case study, we conducted interviews with four columnists and editors in *Nordlys* and two editors in competing media in the region (five men and one woman). We conducted content analyses of editorial columns and audience contributions. These studies were first concerned with printed formats, then the transition to online versions. Both raised new questions as the genre continues to develop into new formats, such as podcasts, and we decided to make a follow-up study of opinionated journalism podcasts.

Our most recent study consisted of qualitative interviews with seven Norwegian columnists who also worked with podcasts. This part of the study was carried out during the winter of 2020/2021 and consisted of three male and four female participants. The participants were strategically selected due to the podcasts they worked with to represent four different newsrooms. The study also included a qualitative analysis of the podcasts these columnists worked on.

The three studies are closely connected, as the second was a follow-up to the first, and each study built on the others. In total, we interviewed 25 different columnists and editors (five of whom were interviewed in several of the projects). Although all our studies entailed content analysis, text analysis, and interviews, this chapter is based solely on our interviews with columnists. The text analysis of the podcasts is discussed in a separate article (see Morlandstø and Mathisen, submitted, 2021). In this chapter, we predominantly focus on the interview data from our recent study. We use the former two studies to elaborate changes in the columnists' professional perceptions and experiences in order to discuss how genre development impacts on the columnists' professional roles. We conducted three of these recent interviews face to face, with the remainder conducted on Microsoft Teams because of the COVID-19 pandemic. We transcribed and coded responses to the questions in the interview guide, supplementing our analysis with additional in vivo codes (Manning, 2017).

The discussion of our findings concentrates on three main aspects. First, we elaborate on some characteristics: how the columnists' work is organized as well as their motivations to become columnists. Second, we discuss motivation, autonomy in work, and empowerment. Third, we discuss new formats of commentary journalism and their implications for the professional role, addressing aspects of branding, among others.

Highly educated and motivated

As previously stated, the participant sample of our recent (2021) study included female and male columnists representing different regional and national media companies. They represented a highly educated core: one holds a PhD, and most of them have master's degrees. They had backgrounds as political journalists, cultural journalists, or foreign correspondents, and were for the most part experienced journalists before entering the commentary genre.

Except for one self-employed informant, all participants worked in separate columnist departments in their media companies, which constitutes the essential separation between 'news' and 'views' in journalism. Most of the informants produce personal signed columns that are published daily in print and online. They all work with podcasts, some were involved in relatively new ventures, and some have done it for years. Two of them worked primarily with podcasts at the time of the study.

It is also interesting to note that our recent respondents are relatively young: three of them were in their early 30s, one was 43, two of them were 50, and one was 61. In our first study in 2013, several of the informants problematized the idea that most columnists were men close to the age of retirement, and they were worried about future recruiting. As one of them stated in the 2013 interviews, 'Young journalists seem to lack the interest in working with opinionated journalism'. Eight years later, we found an increased interest and rather young newly recruited journalists, which indicates good recruiting potential. We also observed that the number of female columnists had increased.

Both in 2021 and 2013, we asked the columnists to describe a typical working week according to the amount of work they produced. With little variation, they produced between three and five texts per week in addition to their podcasts in 2021. Three of the podcasts were published weekly, one daily. Based on their own descriptions, we might conclude that the work of columnists is not characterized as the hastiest and most time-pressured part of journalistic production. One of them elaborated:

> Compared to the amount of stories I produced as a news journalist, I find my commentary production rather small (…) I often think that I can't really understand how media companies can afford having employees that hardly write.

We heard similar descriptions regarding the amount of work in our other 2013 interviews as well. Hasty and superficial hamster-wheel journalism (Nygren, 2008; Lee-Wright et al., 2012) does not fit the working conditions for a columnist. On the contrary, the commentators described quite a thorough and demanding research process as a vital part of working with columns, in order to keep themselves updated and to control the facts they build upon. One of the informants in 2021 stated:

> I try to be a source-based commentator. I spend quite a lot of time in the field, travelling around in the region, meeting people, talking to people, listening to people. I walk in the corridors of Parliament. I read.

They all describe extensive reading of documents, reports, books and dissertations, background conversations, and participating in conferences and political meetings. 'It is important to keep updated' and to 'talk to people that know more than yourself', two of them underlined. Another interviewee described how as a commentator she needed to constantly *monitor* the news agenda instead of *driving* it, which she did as a reporter. The informants in our first study underlined similarly thorough work with research and sources. As one of them stated in 2013, 'I do read a lot – books, journals, newspapers, online resources. You have to be continuously updated in public debate'. These descriptions do not substantiate the perception of cheap journalism. We find that these kinds of work perceptions are unchanged from 2013 to 2021 and might be described as one of the stable aspects of opinionated journalism.

When describing their motivation to work as commentators and analysts rather than reporters, several of the 2021 sample had been encouraged by their editors to apply for such a position or were actively recruited into it. Regarding their own motivations, the possibility to express opinions and work with analytical journalism emerged as essential. One of them, a former political journalist, stated, 'The analytical part of the job was the most tempting. The possibility to explain, to give meaning'. Another said, 'I wanted to be an actor myself, not just mediate the opinions of other people'. This respondent was a former political journalist in a print-oriented newspaper. He contemplated his job shift with a desire to work more online and develop his digital skills, as his present employer is a more digital-oriented newsroom. Statements such as 'a need to express my own opinions' and 'it gave me a possibility to work with a more free and autonomous style and rhetoric' underline that primarily, these commentators' motivations are rooted in a need and desire to analyze, interpret, and express opinions rather than merely report. Similarly, the informants in our first study were motivated in their jobs in similar ways, with utterances such as 'to contextualize news flow and politics', 'to stimulate public debate and civic engagement', and to 'be analytical'. Being a columnist offers the possibility to advance professional skills other than being a political journalist or news reporter, and this kind of motivation seemed unchanged during these eight years.

Not surprisingly, as shown in the quotations above, the columnists found the possibility to express meaning and be analytical as the most professionally satisfying aspect of their jobs. Formulations such as 'to advance my rhetorical style', 'define the context above the single case, story or incident', and 'I really want to be an active part in the public debate in society' yet again substantiate the desire for working with a more opinionated and analytical approach. We found similar explanations in 2013, with ideas such as 'I like to participate in the societal debate and give citizens new perspectives' and 'I want to make politics interesting and understandable to citizens and audiences'.

However, our participants also experienced some challenging aspects of their work, challenges that we have observed since 2013. All of them underlined the fear of misunderstanding, or of expressing disinformation. As one stated, 'What I fear most is presenting wrong facts or failing with the source criticism'. All informants described a similar fear of disclosure: 'You are personally responsible for what you write; you can't hide behind the sources', said one of them. They also feel a responsibility to represent their newsrooms, that disinformation or poor source criticism would damage not only their own professional reputations but the trustworthiness of the entire newsroom. Still, they underlined freedom in work – an aspect we explore and develop further in the next section, as autonomy is a vital concept in this volume.

Autonomy and empowered positions

For professions, the notion of autonomy is a central ideal. On the institutional level, autonomy refers to the ideal that the institution of journalism should act as an independent force in society, exercising professional discretion free from external impact. The dissolution of the party press foregrounds such autonomy, giving way to a more critical journalism where personal columns become more important on behalf of the editorial. At the individual level, autonomy refers to the journalist's ability to define the content of their own work. This phenomenon is of most vital interest here.

All the 2021 interviewees described that they perceived the rather high freedom to decide their own working hours as being related to several aspects. One mentioned the content of work, or more precisely what topics and questions they could write about. Others found that 'We have blanket authority regarding issues; no one asks what we are doing'. Another respondent explained:

> This really is a luxury job. We are free to write about exactly what we desire. In a way, we might cherry-pick the good cases and stories other journalists have dug out and choose what we will go into, interpret and view opinions about.

Such perceptions of *luxury, incredible freedom,* and *the ability to cherry pick* were substantiated by all informants, who underlined the 'freedom to travel and meet people' and 'the possibility to work with issues I burn for'. One of them drew lines back to the party press, describing his present work as characterized by 'a lot of freedom now'.

The informants described perceived freedoms related to what they deal with in their columns and podcasts, as well as how to organize their working days; how they work with research; which conferences and meetings to participate in; and the ability to go out in the field, meet people, and have conversations with them. This kind of autonomy is related to the content and procedures of their everyday work. We also found similar perceptions of freedom in our 2013 and 2015 studies. We characterize a perception of professional autonomy as an essential characteristic of one's role as a columnist.

Our respondents also acknowledged that they hold a kind of societal power in public debate, having an impact on opinion-forming processes in society. One of them stated:

> The issues and themes we set on the agenda gain public attention (...). To a certain degree, we might impact the public opinion in a specific issue. (...) Perhaps most important is the possibility to focus on specific cases and issues. I think that impacts upon the entire societal debate, and might influence important decisions.

Several underlined the power in having continuous access to wide-reaching platforms and large newspapers where their analysis could be read and their voices heard. One stated that she felt more empowered as a commentator than she had been as a news reporter. She experienced that her words could hit hard and that people sometimes felt offended and aggrieved because of things she had written. However, one interviewee emphasized that the line between power and powerlessness might be thin:

> I have influencing power, yes. However, I am also powerless because it is easy to write banalities. And when you do that, it really doesn't

work well. As a columnist, you don't have the power to force reality into your tracks. However, you have the power to frame the discussion, which in itself is rather important.

Moreover, in 2013 when the columns went from being 'printed gold' to being published freely online, the informants underlined the power in having public access. However, in 2013, the informants were more reserved in their perceptions of having societal power as professional columnists. In 2013, several of our informants answered 'no' when we asked them whether they experienced power as columnists. One of them said, 'No, I have not. It is the politicians that have power. What I write does not have any consequences, but I am one of many voices contributing to public debate'. Some informants experienced power in 2013, but in 2021 all of the informants seemed more conscious about the societal power they held. It seems that admitting one has power is more accepted in 2021 than eight years earlier. Several explanations might be behind this change. First, our 2013 study was closer in time to several critical public debates regarding the role of columnists in political scandals. This might have led to columnists' need to defend their role, toning down their societal impact. Further, we might discuss whether this more unreservedly expressed perception of power in 2021 might be related to constant and steady growth: newsrooms increasingly prioritize columnist departments, which underline professional self-confidence as well as the increased prestige and status of being a columnist. It might also be interpreted in terms of boundary disputes: acknowledging societal power constitutes the demarcation of professional journalism and highlights its societal value. We will return to this aspect later in the chapter when discussing how columnists perceive social media.

Digital rehearsal, dialogue, and playfulness

So far in this chapter, we have elaborated characteristics of the professional role of columnists. Commentary journalism is a genre with roots which stretch back centuries and was developed in the era of the printed press. Digitalization has transferred the genre into new formats. First, columns have gone from printed versions onto media companies' digital platforms. Second, social media has become an essential channel for distribution and promotion, as opinionated texts stimulate shares and likes (Mathisen and Morlandstø, 2018). These have also increased the expectation of columnists to communicate with and participate in social media debates with their readers. Third, the migration to digital has also helped the genre innovate and develop into new formats and styles (Morlandstø and Mathisen, 2016). Among these, the podcast is essential, in line with the increasing popularity of podcasts in a diverse range of genres (Berry, 2016). Our aim is to elaborate how these transformations of genre impact on the role of columnists.

First, we find that when the commentary genre shifted to digital platforms, the *dialogical aspect* of the commentaries was strengthened. Commentary journalism might be traditionally described as authoritative and serious, often dealing with politics. In the printed era, it was also characterized by a monological style, where columnists sat on their pedestals or in their 'ivory towers', as one of our 2013 informants explained it, talking *to* and not *with* the citizens and audiences. Digitalization changed that. The informants described their process of climbing down from their pedestals as wholly positive, enhancing democracy and public debate. The new formats of commentating entail a more discourse-based commentary. In podcasts, several columnists participate in each episode, conversing with each other. One of our 2021 informants emphasized the need for dialogue:

> The time we live in needs conversation more than monologue. And I find the podcast a beautiful point of departure for conversation, and for stimulating conversations elsewhere also.

The dialogue replaces the monologue, which also gives more space for provision, reflection, and doubts than more beefy utterances. Thus, the new formats of commentating entail a more discourse-based commentary. The columnist is still an 'opinionist', creating meaning, but they also turn more into a conversation partner, guiding listeners through societal and political matters as an intellectual discussant.

Second, the internet and social media have changed communications in the public sphere as well. Columnists are challenged by social media influencers and bloggers. Social media has become vital for the distribution of columns. One 2021 informant described how commentary journalism is increasingly challenged by social media influencers, which she finds has been a boon to commentary journalism: 'These trends have benefitted good commentary journalism, because it can't be unprecise and without substance'. Another informant marked the difference between professional columnists and social media debaters this way:

> Our work is rooted in press ethics, which is not the fact for everybody in social media. We are bound to a profession, professional and ethical norms. (…) We represent a form of quality assurance of both the facts and statements we bring than other debaters do (…) Thus, what the newsroom presents is perceived to be more trustworthy.

Both of these statements can be interpreted as boundary work (see Gieryn, 1983; Carlson, 2015), where the professionals are drawing a line separating themselves from influencers and other opinionated actors in the public sphere. They stress that commentary journalism conveys substance, quality, and a standard that other sources do not entail. They note that the columnists have their place within the professional community, while bloggers and influencers are left outside professional borders. In 2013, most of our informants were very optimistic about how digitalization and social media might impact their work as well as the societal debate. They used words like 'enriching' and 'a huge democratization' and emphasized increased possibilities for dialogue between columnists and their audience. They also underlined the value of contradictory perceptions nuancing their perspectives: 'It is really time that we who express our opinions in public meet counter-voices and resistance', said one of them. Eight years later, columnists still value the democratic value of broad civic participation; however, it seems as though the need to demarcate between journalistic commentaries and other forms for voicing opinions in public debate are more urgent. Columnists feel responsible for stimulating a healthy public debate, and they find that their professional standards for research better equip them to do so than ordinary social media influencers.

Third, working with new formats also creates possibilities to *enhance professional skills* in new areas. One respondent stated:

> The podcast functions as a part of the digitalization of the newsroom, and a professionalization of the commentator department as media actors. You get practice in acting in front of camera and microphone. (…) The podcast is a tool to professionalize the newsroom within broadcast.

A similar description is this: 'The podcast represents a kind of rehearsal project in working with audio for us writing-based columnists'. These observations illustrate how old genres are developed into new formats suited to the digital media landscape, and that newsroom development is another means to develop and increase professionals' digital skills (Mathisen and Morlandstø, 2018, p. 42). Engaging with innovative ventures such as podcasts often implies autonomy and creativity in work.

In the 2015 study, we elaborated on two specific cases of genre development: *Brif* in *Bergens Tidende* (explanatory journalism; Morlandstø and Mathisen, 2017) and *Nordnorsk debatt* in *Nordlys* (Mathisen and Morlandstø, 2018). Several of our 2015 informants concluded that participating in innovative ventures contributes to increased job satisfaction, stimulating a feeling of empowerment, professional contentedness, and maturation. The professionals involved in these two cases perceived change as a necessity and conveyed an adaptive attitude, using concepts such as *eternal process, constantly changing, unfinished, in a development phase, laboratory*, and *hatchery* when describing their work. One of them stated, 'We have succeeded in making *Brif* a hatchery for how to present good and relevant journalism in the new digital media environment'. Thus, being part of this developing work can also be seen as part of multiskilling, which allows greater autonomy (Nygren, 2014). It might empower the participants to engender their skills and competencies, sustaining their status as desirable employees.

Moving on to the 2021 case, several of our informants highlighted that podcasts represent commentary journalism in a new form, one in which *entertainment* has becomes a more vital aspect:

> I think we all are aiming to let ourselves out more, be more free and forward (…) the podcast does not represent mere entertainment, and still deals with serious topics; however, it perhaps exists in the borderland between commentary and entertainment.

Another participant described a similar experience: 'It is less formal, down-to-earth, lowering the shoulders, (…) kind of twaddling, more playful'. His colleague reflected in the same direction about how the podcast contributes to a freer form of commentary:

> Maybe the podcast has broken down some of the gravity and seriousness in journalism (…) Of course we want to be perceived as a serious and trustworthy actor, and we will continue along that line. However, if we only become grey, dull and serious, people do not subscribe to us.

One of the columnists compared the collegial discussion in the podcast to being as if 'the listeners are invited to have a Friday afternoon beer with us'. Another observed, 'It's quite a long distance between the serious and formal tone of voice in the editorials to the tone of voice in the podcast'. The innovation and development of the commentary genre, most recently by the commentary podcast, has emerged as an augmentation to societal communication.

Through podcasts, the columnists fulfil the role of a funny mate, acting out previous dialogues with colleagues in a cheerful way, giving room for humour and nonsense. The funny mate challenges and dares the audience, with a glint in their eye. The role of a cheerful mate also contributes to the more personalized role of a columnist, where the columnist becomes more visible and exposed than before. In the podcast, they talk about their sexual orientation, their political affiliation, their pregnancies, births, and childhood experiences. Such personalization leads us to a discussion of branding and celebrities.

Branded goods and celebrities

Advancing their digital and oral skills of course empowers the commentators and contributes to their multiskilling development. However, it also fulfils the managers' desires. Columnists have long been valued as prized assets of media companies. Transferring their commentary to the podcast genre has not changed this. On the contrary, it has reinforced their branding role. When a podcast is seen as a means to strengthen the oral competence of the commentators, this will also increase their ability to perform in debate programs and panels, in live broadcasts. For print-based columnists, the podcast serves as a tool to advance their ability to perform live and express themselves orally. Several of the informants brought up the expectations they had met to be heard and seen, and to be able to enter prestigious national debates. One of them recalled:

> For management, the aim was clearly to be more visible in the national public sphere. (…) it's a spoken and stated ambition from management, an order to bring up our newsroom in the national sphere. We commentators are expected to be heard and seen in other media than our own.

Statements like this substantiate the same perception that a podcast also serves as a tool for a columnist's personal profiling and branding:

> It's a stronger personal profiling than in earlier days. However, (…) when I was a boy, you also knew who the profiled commentators were. But there are more of us now, and the pressure is stronger because you have the impact of the 24/7 news cycle. I think the accelerating speed in news journalism is essential for this development.

Working with podcasts undoubtedly contributes to columnists' multiskilling and thus makes them even more valuable as professionals and employees. Multiskilling and empowering participation in innovative work in many ways follow a professional logic, contributing to re-professionalization. However, they also reveal an underlying market logic (Freidson, 2001; Nygren, 2008), as columnists are expected to be seen and heard and participate in prestigious debate programs. The commercial considerations activated here are not related to revenue streams or income, but rather to overall branding. Visibility and profiling create online traffic, attract readers and audiences, and contribute to the media company's branding.

Already in the 2013 interviews, we found attention paid to branding, exemplified in statements like 'commentary journalism may contribute to a branding loyalty that is essential for us as a media company'. In the 2015 case studies, the focus on branding strengthened, as informants drew our attention to the commercial and marketing potential of the innovations. They used words and concepts such as *branding, building audience loyalty, increasing online traffic,* and *capturing new audience groups* – commercial concepts more easily associated with the language of marketers than with newsroom practitioners. One of the editors describes the columns as premium or quality content:

> We have to profile our columnists as branded goods to a larger degree than we used to (…). Branding creates digital engagement and audience loyalty. This represents a core value of our business.

The celebrifying of columnists and their value as branded goods represents nothing new, as such. However, it seems as though the digitization and transforming of the genre into new formats strengthens these foci. Profiled columnists are still legitimized in the societal role of journalism, contributing to and stimulating an enlightened and healthy public debate, despite critical voices (Lysbakken and Isaksen, 2008). In parallel, columnists have become an even more vital means to build a brand and claim a visible, profiled place in public debate. In this place, they let the audience into their personal spheres. Columnists enjoy high prestige, which goes hand in hand with an increased responsibility for claiming a profiled sphere in public and acting on several platforms on behalf of the media company where they are employed.

Change and stability

By representing a societal institution, opinionated journalism serves democracy and public discourse. In this chapter, our aims were to discuss what characterizes the professional role of the commentary journalist, then to discuss how the transformation of the commentary genre into new formats affects this role. Regarding the first aim, we find that the columnists under study compose a highly educated core that enjoys freedom in work and acknowledges few constraints. Columnists are given individual space as professionals, using their professional discretion. Even if they experience constraints, they also are empowered to add new routines and practices (Cook, 1998). Thus, the professional life of a columnist is characterized by autonomy, which according to Deuze (2005) represents a building block of journalists' professional identity. Regarding the tension between precarity and autonomy addressed in Chapter 1, we find little trace of precarity and uncertainty. Columnists seem to have a solid place at the opposite end of the spectrum. They also experience a form of societal power and feel a responsibility to contribute to a healthy and enlightened public debate, which confirms the altruistic aspect of professionalism.

Regarding the second aim, columnists perceive that taking part in innovative developments and transferring the commentary genre into new formats demanding multiple technologies improve their skills. In 2021, working on a podcast offers multiskilling possibilities and contributes to re-professionalization, as the genre innovation projects did in 2015. In the socially stratified field of journalism, columnists have traditionally enjoyed prestige and privileges. The innovative venture of commentary journalism has even reinforced this, presenting columnists as multiskilled professionals who are armed to meet future technological changes and are valuable as employees. Thus, the development even strengthens their position in the field. Columnists have long been placed in the more prestigious part of the journalistic field, and they still are a privileged part of the core (Hovden, 2008; Raabe, 2018). Climbing down the ivory tower and facilitating a dialogical debate rather than monological lecturing does not seem to affect their professional status. In the shifting professional landscape, columnists seem to have reinforced their prestigious and empowered positions.

However, they are also increasingly conquered by market logic. They feel a heavy responsibility on their shoulders to represent media outlets with strong traditions. The new formats also entail a more entertaining, profiled, personalized, and celebrated professional role. On the one hand, this confirms their privileged professional position. On the other, increased profiling might also be demanding, and the market logic might challenge professional autonomy (Freidson, 2001; Nygren, 2008).

Thus, commentary journalism is experiencing both change and stability. The stability lies in representing a professional role with long historical roots and tradition, and the societal role to facilitate debate in the public sphere continues to be valued and acknowledged. Columnists' role stability also lies in a longstanding process wherein change in itself is normal: the dissolution of the party press, for example, paved the way for a more independent and personalized role for columnists, and genre innovations on digital platforms have reinforced this.

At the same time, commentary journalism is experiencing change and disruptive forces. Institutionalism is well suited to explain change if it 'captures the way in which old institutions are challenged or repudiated, and new institutions are invented', according to Ryfe (2016, p. 371). Digitalization, the rise of social media, and fragmentation of audiences and the public sphere of course challenge the role of columnists as both facilitators of the public sphere and societal experts. When the public sphere is fragmented, shared frames of reference vanish, and columnists' interpretations and analyses are challenged by a diverse range of independent citizen voices and influencers in social media and blogs.

The agenda-setting power of traditional media and columnists has clearly been disrupted. Within the institutional framework, this disruption might be defined as a critical juncture or a shock. Out of this shock and trembling, a new practice arose, with new formats such as the commentary podcast. Embodying new formats, forms, and tones, the podcast format is a means to capture new audience segments and reinforce the societal role of commentary journalism. However, this new practice is anchored in both market logic and professional logic. For their media companies, highly profiled columnists represent important branding. For the columnists themselves, this amplifies their professional status and transforms them into celebrities, which also reinforces their value as employees.

Within the framework of professional theory, we also see that the changes trigger boundary work. The columnists are demarcating the boundary between professional, knowledge-based, and substantial commentary published within the ethical framework of the press on the one side, and more fragmented utterances of diverging quality on the other – citizen/audience opinion pieces/blogging/social media debate. By drawing such a line, columnists both substantiate how they differ from other actors debating on social media and underline the societal need for their professional opinion-based analysis and interpretations.

These trends exceed commentators' professional role alone, adding new aspects to it. Traditionally, columnists were a kind of societal expert (and they still are), a role that includes being a critical, opinionated voice in society. This function is even amplified by their increasing visibility and performance on prestigious debate programs. They also serve as the readers' guide or educator – a task they have traditionally fulfilled that is rooted in the ideals of enlightening and education. In the fragmented public media sphere, the commentators themselves draw attention to this responsibility to guide, enlighten, and contribute to a lively and healthy public debate. Media logic increases their worth as branded goods for media companies and justifies their position and privileges.

The podcast format introduces new tones and ways to perform in several directions: as some podcasts have a more laid-back style, the podcast commentator emerges as a funny and cheerful mate, a person you would like to have a beer and a chat with at the pub on a Friday afternoon. Other podcasts might have a more formal tone; however, the monologue is buried in favour of dialogue. Thus, the podcast commentator also becomes an intellectual discussant, participating in a conversation with their commentator-colleagues as well as the audiences. As such, the role as profiled brand, witty friend, and intellectual discussant is characteristically new, and complements traditional roles. Stability is present: in its core, columnists do the same as columnists have done for decades – they analyze, interpret, argue, and express opinion. They are still placed in a privileged and prestigious position, enjoying authority. Paralleled, critical junctures lead to new practice, where professional roles are exceeded and boundary struggles take place to demarcate the professional space and its societal value.

References

Allern, S. (2010) From party agitators to independent pundits; The changed historical roles of newspaper and television journalists in Norwegian election campaigns. *Northern Light: Film and Media studies Yearbook*, 8(1), pp. 49–67. DOI: https://doi.org/10.1386/nl.8.49_1

Allern, S. and Pollack, E. (2012) Scandalous! The mediated construction of political scandals in four Nordic Countries. Göteborg: Nordicom evaluation scholarship. *Nordiom Review*, 36(1), pp. 5–18.

Bengtsson, M. (2015) Approaches to political commentary in Scandinavia. A call for textual, evaluation scholarship. *Nordiom Review*, 36(1), pp. 5–18.

Berry, R. (2016) Part of the establishment: Reflecting on 10 years of podcasting as an audio medium,. *Convergence: The International Journal of Research into New Media Technologies*, 22(6), pp. 661–671. DOI: 10.1177/1354856516632105

Bro, P. (2008) Folkestyrets nye fyrmester: Da verden blev oplyst af den politiske kommentator. [When the worlds was enlightened by the political commentator]. In Troels, M. and Peter, B. (eds.), Et løft(e) til journalistikken [A promise to journalism] (1 ed., Vol. 1, pp. 185–206). Syddansk Universitetsforlag.

Bro, P. (2012) License to comment. The popularization of a political commentator. *Journalism Studies*, 13(3), pp. 433–446. DOI: 10.1080/1461670X.2011.616407

Carlson, M. (2015) Introduction: The many boundaries of journalism. In Carlson, M. and Lewis, S. (eds.) *Boundaries of Journalism. Professionalism, Practices and Participation*. London and New York: Routledge, pp. 1–19.

Cook, T.E. (1998) *Governing with the News: The News Media as a Political Institution*. Chicago: University of Chicago Press.

Djerf-Pierre, M. and Weibull, L. (2008) From public educator to interpreting ombudsman. Regimes of political journalism in Swedish public service broadcasting, 1925-2005. Strömbäck, J., Ørsten, M. and Aalberg, T. *Communicating Politics. Political communication in the Nordic Countries*. Göteborg: Nordicom, pp. 195–215.

Deuze, M. (2005) What is journalism? Professional identity and ideology of journalists reconsidered. *Journalism*, 6(4), pp. 442–464. DOI: 10.1177/1464884905056815

Duff, A. (2008) Powers in the land? British columnists in the information era. *Journalism Practice*, 2(2), pp. 230–244. DOI: 10.1080/17512780801999386

Esser, F. and Umbricht, A. (2014) The evolution of objective and interpretative journalism in the Western press: Comparing six news systems since the 1960s. *Journalism & Mass Communication Quarterly*, 91(2), pp. 229–249. London: Sage. DOI: 10.1177/1077699014527459

Fink, K. and Schudson, M. (2014) The rise of contextual journalism, 1950s-2000s. *Journalism*, 15(1), pp. 3–20. Sage. DOI: 10.1177/1464884913479015

Freidson, E. (2001) *Professionalism: The Third Logic*. Cambridge: Polity Press.

Gieryn, T.F. (1983) Boundary work and the demarcation of science from nonscience: strains and interests in professional ideologies of scientists. *American Sociological Review*, 48(6), pp. 781–795. https://doi.org/10.2307/2095325

Hedman, U. (2015) J-Tweeters. *Digital Journalism*, 3(2), pp. 279–297. DOI: 10.1080/21670811.2014.897833

Hovden, J.F. (2008) *Profane and sacred: a study of the Norwegian journalistic field*. PhD-thesis, University of Bergen.

Knapskog, K., Iversen, M.H. and Larsen, L.O (2016) The future of interpretative journalism. in Eide, M., Sjøvaag, H. and Larsen, L.O. (eds.) *Digital Challenges and Professional Reorientations: Lessons from Northern Europe*. Bristol, UK and Chicago: Intellect.

Lee-Wright, P., Philips, A. and Witschge, T. (2012) *Changing Journalism*. London and New York. Routledge.

Liestøl, G. and Morrison, A. (2015) The power of place and perspective: sensory media and situated simulations in urban design. In A. de Souza e Silva and M. Sheller (eds.) *Mobility and Locative Media: Mobile Communication in Hybrid Spaces (Changing Mobilities)*. New York: Routledge, pp. 207–223, ISBN 978-1138778139. 12.

Lindgren, M. (2016) Personal narrative journalism and podcasting. *The Radio Journal International Studies in Broadcast and Audio Media*, 14(1), pp. 23–41. DOI: 10.1386/rjao.14.1.23_1

Lysbakken, A. and Isaksen, T.R. (2008) Kommentariatets diktatur. *Samtiden*, 2008(1), pp. 4–15. Oslo: Aschehoug. [the dictatorship of the commentariat]

Manning, J. (2017) In vivo coding. In Matthes, J. (ed.), *The International Encyclopedia of Communication Research Methods*. New York: Wiley-Blackwell. Retrieved from DOI: 10.1002/9781118901731.iecrm0270

Mathisen, B.R. and Morlandstø, L. (2016) *Kommentaren: en sjanger i endring*. Oslo. Cappelen Damm Akademisk. [The commentary – a changing genre].

Mathisen, B.R. and Morlandstø, L. (2018) Genre innovation in regional media. *Sur le journalisme – About Journalism – Sobre Journalism*, 7(2), pp. 36–48.

Mathisen, B.R. and Morlandstø, L. (2019) Covering regional blind spots: Commentary journalism in the regional public sphere. *Nordicom Rewiev*, 40(1), pp. 75–90. DOI: 10.2478/nor-2019-0004

Morlandstø, L. and Mathisen B.R. (2016) Participation and Control. The interaction between editorial staff, technology and users in online commentary journalism. In *Digital Journalism*, 5(6), pp. 791–808. DOI: 10.1080/21670811.2016.

Morlandstø, L. and Mathisen, B.R. (2017) Digitization: Empowering regional media in public. In Waschková Císařová, L. (ed.) *Voice of the Locality: Local Media and Local Audience*. Brno: Munipress, pp. 239–260.

Morlandstø, L. and Mathisen, B.R. (submitted 2021 Podcast – commentary journalism in a digital public. Submitted Journalistica.

McNair, B. (2000) *Journalism and Democracy. An Evaluation of the Political Public Sphere*. Routledge. London.

McNair, B. (2008) I, Columnist. In Franklin, B. (eds.) *Pulling Newspapers Apart. Analyzing Print Journalism*. London: Routledge.

Nimmo, D.D. and Combs, J. (1992) *The Political Pundits*. New York: Praeger Publishers Inc.

Nord, L., Enli, G. and Stúr, E. (2012) Pundits and political scandals. A study of political commentators in Norway and Sweden. In Allern, S. and Pollack, E. (eds.) *Scandalous! The Mediated Construction of Political Scandals in Four Nordic Countries*. Göteborg: Nordicom, pp. 87–102.

Nygren, G. (2008) Yrke på glid: om journalistrollens de-professionalisering [Profession on the Slide: De-professionalization of the Journalistic Role]. Stockholm: SIMO.

Nygren, G. (2014) Multiskilling in the Newsroom: De-skilling or Re-skilling of Journalistic Work? *The Journal of Media Innovations*, 1(2), pp. 76–96.

Olaussen, U. (2018) The celebrified journalist: Journalistic self-promotion and branding in the celebrity constructs on Twitter. *Journalism Studies*, 19, pp. 2379–2399. DOI: 10.1080/1461670X.2017.1349548

Raabe, T. (2018) *The power of political commentators in the age of social media*. Dissertation for the degree of MPhil, Master of Philosophy, Department of Sociology. University of Cambridge.

Rogstad, I. (2016) Is Twitter just rehashing? Intermedia agenda setting between Twitter and mainstream media, in *Journal of Information Technology & Politics*, 13(2), pp. 142–158. DOI: 10.1080/19331681.2016.1160263

Ryfe, D. (2016) News institutions. In Witschge, T., Anderson, C.V., Domingo, D. and Hermida, A. (eds.) *The SAGE Handbook of Digital Journalism*. Los Angeles: SAGE.

Salgado, S. and Strömback, J. (2012) Interpretive journalism: A review of Concepts, operationalizations and key findings. *Journalism*, 13(2), pp. 144–161. Sage. DOI: 10.1177/1464884911427797

Schudson, M. (1995) *The Power of News*. Cambridge: Harvard University press.

Usher, B.(2020) The celebrified columnist and opinion spectacle: Journalism's changing place in networked public spheres. *Journalism*, 22(11), pp. 2836–2854. DOI:10.1177/1464884919897815

6 Both change and stability

Birgit Røe Mathisen

Introduction

In this book, I have raised the question about whether journalism is moving from a safe and stable past to a future in a state of crisis and uncertainty that will harm both the profession and the societal role of journalism. Or are we facing a new phase in the eternal and everlasting development where journalism continually changes and adapts? Does journalism face destruction or hope, refracture or resilience? I also stated that I would argue the latter. Throughout the empirical chapters, together with my fellow authors, I have discussed and problematized trends and precarious developments that change and challenge journalistic autonomy, identity, discretion, and societal roles in ways that we should not overlook or underestimate. Nonetheless, I argue that journalism is a vital profession offering an important, exciting, and satisfying professional life for newcomers in the field now but also in the future. I further suggest that society will recognize and continue to need journalism. In this concluding chapter, I collect the threads from the various empirical chapters so that I can present a final discussion about journalism in the tension between resilience and disruption. I will also repeat that the aim of this volume was not to cover the entire field of journalism but to shed light on some parts of the profession within the Nordic context. Consequently, important parts of journalism are excluded, even if they constitute vital and valuable professional experience. I limited the elaboration to three specific and different tensions, namely 1) *pressures between precarity and autonomy*, 2) *internal sliding in the professional landscape* and 3) *boundary disputes* that I have discussed with the sociology of professions and institutional theory as analytical frameworks. The Norwegian and Nordic contexts comprise the point of departure and empirical ground, but incorporating a broader scope throughout the discussion. In this chapter, I first address the shifting

DOI: 10.4324/9781003144724-6

landscape before turning to the tension between precarity and autonomy, thereafter discussing boundary struggles. Finally, I offer some concluding remarks.

Internal slides and changing landscape

The first tension is related to internal cleavages and class distinctions within the profession. As a profession, journalism is allowed authority, privileges, and legitimacy. To maintain its status, journalism requires that society recognizes its authority as necessary and legitimate. Moreover, being a societal institution journalism depends upon societal recognition, as one of the hallmarks of an institution is a wide acknowledgement of its tasks (Cook, 1998). A key point of an institution is also its durability and resistance to change (Ryfe, 2016). Still, institutional theory might help assess the changes, capture how institutions are challenged and repudiated, and determine which new directions arise from critical junctures or shocks (Ryfe, 2016, p. 380). Disruption as a critical juncture might change the professional landscape of journalism and how journalism is demarcated and framed. Even if representing a societal institution, the journalistic field is no static phenomenon. The professional landscape experiences slides and changes, as it has always done (Schudson, 2013).

Journalism is described as a socially stratified and hierarchical field (Hovden, 2008), with cleavages between its own centre and periphery. In the centre, we find journalists in the large, prestigious newsrooms, most often placed in the capital of Oslo. Local journalists have traditionally suffered from lower prestige. Local journalists themselves express a feeling of inferiority when comparing themselves to journalists in larger newsrooms (Mathisen, 2013), as discussed in Chapter 3. Academic studies have discussed the role of local journalism and shown the low amount of critical reporting involved (Mathisen and Morlandstø, eds, 2019). In addition, digital shifts and metrics have moved local journalism in a direction where the local anchoring loosens (Olsen, 2018). However, one distinct change in scholarly as well as public and political debates in recent years is the increased recognition for local journalism (Waschková Císařová, 2017; Hess and Waller, 2017). White papers and media policy prioritize public support for local media. Political authorities underline the value of strong local journalism. Local journalism is acknowledged and valued by fellow professionals as well as researchers, politicians, and citizens in general. Throughout the country, we also find an increasing tendency toward cooperation across newsrooms on various levels. One example is between the broadcaster NRK and local newspapers during election campaigns. Studies have also shown that local journalists perceive professional autonomy and enjoy high levels of trust in society (Lamark and Morlandstø, 2019). Adding that local media outlets have been remarkably stable during a crisis and downsizing, these trends might contribute to an increased professional self-confidence among local journalists. Thus, as valuing and recognition are enhanced, local journalists might climb up the professional hierarchy, transferring from the periphery to closer to the centre.

Freelancers are another part of the profession that have been placed in the periphery (Hovden, 2008); they are journalists who take assignments from several assigners and are paid by the piece. However, despite experiences of precarious working conditions and job insecurity, freelancing has also received a growing acknowledgement. As the number of freelancers increases in a wide range of countries, it becomes more common as a professional path. Journalism schools in several countries also focus on freelancing in their curricula, considering it important to prepare students for a working life outside of traditional newsrooms. In addition, the union of journalists might demonstrate a more distinct focus, raising discussions related to freelancers' working conditions and rights. Also, the scholarly interest in freelancing has increased remarkably during the last 10–15 years, as discussed in Chapter 4 (see, for example, Gollmitzer, 2014; Cohen, 2016; Mathisen, 2016; Norbäck, 2021). We also see that freelancers enjoy high job satisfaction and experience high professional autonomy, which is one of the building blocks in the professional ideology of journalism (Deuze, 2008).

In addition, the traditional trade press constitutes a stable part of the media landscape, as discussed in Chapter 3. In the 30-year period between 1987 and 2017, the trade press experienced a professionalization process and moved from primarily being information channels for their owners to becoming independent publications, surmounted by the professional standard of press ethics. Thus, the trade press has grown substantially as an employer, regarding journalistic quality and the amount of jobs (Steensen and Kalsnes, 2020, p. 6).

The mapping conducted in Chapter 3 also pictures the diverse media landscape that constitutes the working life of journalists as professionals and suggests several trends. We see examples where journalists from larger newsrooms move to smaller niche media, either as a founder or an employee, and thus transfer to the more fringed part of the profession. As we also saw in Chapter 3, newcomers enter the field and adopt the traditional professional ideals of journalism. New niche media are established and cover thematic niches such as media business and law. Additionally, new hyperlocal outlets emerge, covering what was perceived to be geographical blind spots, both in the capital and rural municipalities.

Within the Norwegian context, the number of journalistic publications and editions has been remarkably stable during years of restructuring, digital transition, and economic losses. However, large newsrooms have shrunk, and fewer jobs are available. From 1987 to 2017, the number of jobs advertised in the trade press publication *Journalisten* had reduced by 50 percent. Most dramatic was the reduction in permanent jobs, whereas short-term contracts emerged as the new standard (Steensen and Kalsnes, 2020). Traditional newsrooms have downsized and employ fewer journalists. For those remaining, work is more intensified, time-constrained, and hasty (Cohen et al., 2019). Still, none of the traditional newsrooms have vanished, they employ a substantial amount of journalists, and they represent stability. Traditional newsrooms also offer their employees the opportunity to develop and innovate the way journalism is being expressed and published (Morlandstø and Mathisen, 2016). For example, the columnists interviewed in Chapter 5 all took part in such developments.

In parallel, however, newcomers also challenge the status quo in the field of journalism (Wagemans et al., 2016), exceeding the profession and making it more diverse. They represent new voices and tones that take journalism in diverse directions. The main reasons for starting a new journalism business include the lack of jobs at existing media companies, the demise of legacy media, and the discontent with existing journalism (Naldi and Picard, 2012). Start-ups might therefore be seen as a form of counterforce, renewing journalism in an investigative and independent direction (Küng, 2015).

We also see a trend where newcomers are rooted in a professional motivation to reinforce journalistic values, as expressed by the interviewees we met in Chapter 3. An example of this is the establishment of the French Mediapart, whose strong journalistic, ideological stance is its strongest asset (Wagemans et al., 2016). This ideological stance can be identified as a return to 'traditional' journalistic values, challenging traditional media organizations and at the same time reinventing the way journalism can be organized (p. 171). In a study among journalistic start-ups in Norway, Iversen (2020) found a similar motivation toward fortifying journalistic values. Her informants are motivated by professionalism, and they protect their journalistic identity. Thus, they contribute to professionalism and to a re-professionalization of journalism, and at the same time they also extend and exceed the professional landscape, making it more diverse and multifaceted.

Here, we can also take a quick sidestep toward the range of journalistic counter-movements that have emerged in recent years, aiming to correct a media logic driving journalism in a hasty and superficial direction. Slow journalism, explanatory journalism, constructive journalism, and solutions journalism are all examples of these kinds of counter-discourses, drawing from journalism's traditional core values related to storytelling, education, and quality. These kinds of counter-movements are seen as a reaction to speed and real-time reporting that damage accuracy and quality in journalism. They bring in other discourses and challenge the mindsets and procedures of work in journalism. One could question whether slow journalism is mostly an elitist and nostalgic project, however, these kinds of counter-movements do not imagine themselves to be a replacement for fast journalism or as the future. Their small-scale independence allows freedom from mainstream journalism organizations and their competitive drive for profit and ideology of journalistic velocity (LeMasurier, 2015, p. 148).

We see trends suggesting that groups that have traditionally been situated in the periphery are slowly moving, experiencing increasing prestige and recognition. In parallel, there are fewer employed journalists in the larger newsrooms, and the traditional core is decreasing. These trends underline the fact that the profession of journalism slides and changes. Still, it represents persistence where professional values and ideals are reinforced. In other words, it is a kind of stability. Despite disruption and critical junctures, the newsrooms remain, develop, innovate, employ journalists, and represent vital arenas where professional identity is built and reinforced.

Precarity and autonomy

In this strain between change and stability, a significant internal cleavage or class distinction comes with the tension between precarity and autonomy. Precarious work has emerged as a serious challenge and a major concern in the contemporary world, with widespread consequences (Kalleberg, 2018, p. 3). Being a societal institution, journalism is closely connected to other institutions and depends on exterior framework conditions that impact professionals on the inside. Governments and businesses have sought to make labour markets more flexible to compete in an increasingly competitive world economy (Kalleberg, 2018, p. 4). Neoliberal globalization has propelled the spread of precarious employment, and new digital publishing models are emerging faster than their implications for journalists and journalism can be fully understood (Cohen, 2016, p. 5). This ongoing precarization of journalism makes it more unstable, uncertain, and unsecure (Kalleberg and Vallas, 2018).

In Chapter 4, we discussed how freelancers, despite high job satisfaction, suffer from uncertainty, precarious working conditions, and low income. Even in the framework of the Nordic work-life model (Hvid and Falkum, 2019), with its safety net, regulations, and high union density, freelancing appears a risky business. Precariousness not only affects traditional freelancers. In job ads, the number of regular positions in journalism has decreased, and employers increasingly offer temporarily positions and short-term contracts (Steensen and Kalsnes, 2020). Journalists working in start-ups and new niche media in Chapter 3 also experienced uncertainty in their work.

A significant division in the professional landscape is between those in unsecure, precarious conditions, facing an uncertain future, and those in safe, regular positions (Wiik, 2015). This might be characterized as a breaking up of the profession from within, where increasing differences between journalists are related to work content, salaries, and form of employment. The workforce is divided into a 'core staff' that gives the company its profile on the one hand and temporarily employ journalists on the other (Witschge and Nygren, 2009, p. 50).

The highly valued columnists might stand as an example of those enjoying professional prestige and empowerment in public debate, whereas freelancers often suffer from precarity. The professional lives of columnists in rather large, legacy newsrooms and single freelancers differ in many ways, most of all related to job and economic safety. Chapters 4 and 5, however, also include some interesting parallels between these two professional groups. The freelancers and columnists participating in these two studies are highly educated and stand out as competent professionals. They both enjoy high job satisfaction. They both perceive autonomy in daily work and experience a range of developing and advancing professional possibilities. For both groups there is an emotional attachment to their jobs, and journalism seems to be a path for professional realization.

However, despite these positive aspects, both groups also face commercial constraints, experiencing external commercial and economic forces impacting on their professional lives. For freelancers, these constraints are obviously connected to bad pay, low income, and the difficulties maintaining a balance between work and leisure. They are always ready to jump in and will rarely decline an assignment. However, the prestigious commentariat also face commercial challenges in daily work, expressed through increasing expectations to be profiled and visible in public debate. Profiled columnists have always been regarded as brands for their media companies. In the digitized media landscape, this aspect is strongly underlined. As social media is important for sharing and distributing editorial content, columnists expressing distinct and controversial opinions contribute to likes, shares, and comments, and thus the profiling of the news company as a brand. Developing the commentary genre on new platforms comprises possibilities to advance one's professional and multiskilling capacities for those involved. At the same time, columnists have become celebrities and personalized brands. These expectations can hardly be described as a precarious aspect of work; however, they are commercial and stand as an example of how the contemporary crisis in the journalism industry has necessitated a re-evaluation of the editorial–finance relationship (Rafter, 2016, p. 140).

The tension between autonomy and precarity also involves entrepreneurialism. The disruption of journalism has made entrepreneurial journalism a vital topic in industry and education. Of course, entrepreneurialism in journalism isn't anything new. The history of journalism is marked by an entrepreneurial spirit from its beginning (Rafter, 2016). However, it is important to reflect on how we view, interpret, and talk about entrepreneurialism in the neoliberal working life. The counterpart of entrepreneurialism might in many ways be precarity, constituting two contrasting perceptions on how working life develops: the discourse about entrepreneurialism versus the discourse about the precarious and marginalized worker (Smeaton, 2003).

On the one hand, entrepreneurship is an ideal type of self-employment that enables individuals to control their labour process, an idealized vision of 'portfolio' or boundaryless careers, including flexibility and autonomy (Cohen, 2016, p. 10). The portfolio perception sees free agency as liberating and a move away from alienating bureaucratic control toward independence as well as sovereignty over time and tasks (Smeaton, 2003, p. 380). However, this might obscure more than it reveals, as the underside of a portfolio career is uncertainty, insecurity, and lack of control. Temporarily, casual work colonizes more of life, and boundaryless is often an obfuscating gloss on precarity (Cohen, 2016, p. 13). The new self-employed are largely economic refugees, affected by downsizing and staff-cutting, and suffering from low earnings and a 'feast or famine' flow of work (Smeaton, 2003, p. 381), where working life is uncertain and individualized (Beck, 2000). The rise of precariousness is linked to the erosion of union strength and power (Cohen, 2016; Vallas and Christin, 2018).

Words and concepts are not insignificant, and it is important to reflect upon how we view this development, both in professional debates and journalism school classes. Of course, entrepreneurialism offers professional possibilities and even makes room for newcomers to strengthen professional values as a reaction to hasty hamster-wheel journalism. Entrepreneurialism might in many ways make the professional landscape more diverse and create new publications offering a wide range of voices and perceptions of reality accessible in the public sphere. On the other hand, it constitutes a riskier and more precarious working life for journalists inside the professional landscape. It transfers risk and responsibility from the employer to the single journalists. Professional life becomes increasingly individualized, vaporizing collective rights.

Boundary disputes

This brings us further to the next tension: who is perceived to be inside the professional community? The sliding landscape might also evoke new boundary disputes. Boundary work is about the legitimate power to define, describe, and explain (Carlson, 2015). Thus, boundary work might also be seen as a struggle for autonomy, securing professional jurisdiction or control over what is regarded as pure and decent professional work. The disruption also affects how the hallmarks of journalism are shaped, constituted, and negotiated. How is journalism understood, how is it limited, who is perceived to be a journalist, and who is judged and kept outside the professional community? Those we consider to be journalists might change as 'technologies of news relay broaden the field of who might be considered a journalist and what might be considered journalism' (Zelizer, 2004, p. 23).

The agenda-setting power of journalists in societal communication is disrupted, and the division between journalists, bloggers, and social media influencers is blurred. In Chapter 5, we saw how the columnists marked the border between professional columnists and other opinion-giving voices, such as bloggers and influencers. We also suggest a trend where this kind of protection has become more distinctive across the years. While hallmarks are blurred and the agenda-setting power of columnists is challenged and vaporized, it is asserted that the professional columnist guarantees a quality that other forms of expression do not offer. Newsrooms prioritize opinion-ated journalism, and interpretative and opinionated journalism increases. As a societal institution, journalism depends on being acknowledged and legitimated for fulfilling a societal need. When columnists' status as facili-tators of public debate is threatened, it becomes mandatory to protect and define the borders between professional columnists and other opinion-giv-ing voices, as well as legitimize the role of professional columnists; that is, society needs independent columnists to interpret and create order in a fragmented public.

Journalism is becoming a permanent desk job, where the work is concentrated in the newsroom with less time in the field (Witschge and Nygren, 2009, p. 43). The rapid changes in media work partly reflect the changing competences and skills that journalists require. When newsrooms apply for new employees, they not only seek out journalists but digital developers and multimedia competence. 'Journalists are confronted with a new reality that requires new skill sets, competencies and knowledge they previously didn't possess' (Guo and Volz, 2019, p. 1294). Use of the word 'journalist' has decreased in job ads, whereas concepts such as content producer have become more common as a range of content-marketing bureaus have been established (Steensen and Kalsnes, 2020, p. 14). On the one hand, this might lead to the professional field expanding and journalism as professional work embracing a larger variety of competencies. On the other hand, it also might dilute journalistic identity and blur the borders between journalism and marketing (Guo and Volz, 2019, p. 1309).

Boundary work also affects which logics control the work, as well as the professional or commercial logic, as discussed in Chapter 2. Cohen, Hunter, and O'Donnell (2019, p. 583) describe a commodification of journalism, where circulation and distribution become key elements of journalistic work and reorient journalists toward the market and commercial values, where journalists feel individually responsible for the profitability of their company. In Chapter 5, we saw that columnists, despite a high degree of autonomy in their work, also experience the expectation of being visible and exposed in public debate and contributing to the media company's branding. Commentary journalism is highly prioritized, developed, and innovated, which is a trend the newsroom has legitimated out of a societal need and public purpose. At the same time, commercial considerations are present. Editorial and commercial considerations seem to go hand in hand when journalism is developed (Morlandstø and Mathisen, 2016).

Boundary work is also essential when discussing freelancers. In Chapter 4, we saw that many freelancers combine journalistic assignments with work in the sector of PR and communication. We also observed that freelancers combining these elements were more eager to leave media work, and they struggled more with the work-leisure balance than those who only accepted pure journalistic assignments. This combination might blur and challenge the borders of journalism. Thus, economic aspects and working conditions also impact on how the demarcation lines are drawn, as well as how they are legitimized.

In Chapters 1 and 2, I also addressed the Norwegian debate regarding union membership. In 1997, the union restricted its borders and expelled 150 members because they worked within the communication sector. The union made a resolution that rules of membership did not allow professionals working in PR and communication to become part of the professional community. Still, many freelancers have been operating in both zones and kept their membership. Twenty-four years later, a new proposal has been raised aiming to open up and loosen the borders, with the reduced number of union members constituting a vital background. The suggestion will also introduce a wide range of competencies in the journalistic community and exceed the current perception of journalistic work. Both in 1997 and 2021, these proposals evoked debates, protests, and support, which put the soul of journalism at stake. Both of these debates illustrate how the shaping of boundaries isn't unaffected by exterior forces and societal development. Via boundary disputes, the profession aims to reinforce professional control and claim authority. Still, disruption and change also push at how the profession draws demarcation lines and defines its borders.

As this Norwegian debate was still in its early phases at the conclusion of this manuscript, future research should focus on following this and similar debates in other countries as vital themes. Which arguments are brought forth, which viewpoints and stands are taken, which parts argue for the liberalization of membership rules, and which part of the profession argues for continuity of the existing? These kinds of questions will bring essential knowledge about how boundary struggles are conducted, as well as how an existing professional landscape slides, stretches, expands, or limits.

Concluding remarks

The profession of journalists has experienced critical junctures and shocks. Borders have become blurred and challenge our understanding of who are regarded as journalists. Still, there is a distinct stability where the core of professional values and ideals is reinforced and strengthened. Newcomers and journalists outside established newsrooms might challenge and force the profession into the fringes. However, they might also adopt an even more fortified professional identity, as many of them are basically driven by a desire to fill blind spots and produce journalism that is in line with professional ideals. They also exceed the profession. In many ways, the development might contribute to a re-professionalization rather than a de-professionalization.

However, the professional landscape comprises several class distinctions and cleavage lines, with perhaps the most serious being that connected to working conditions. A fundamental line is drawn between those on insecure and precarious job conditions, and those enjoying job security, prestige, and high wages. When journalists consider leaving, working conditions seem to be one important trigger. Thus, working conditions seem to be of fundamental significance for how the profession of journalists will develop in the future: reinforcing its resilience or moving towards destruction. Returning to Schudson's (2013) and Broersma's (2013) diverging perception on journalism discussed in Chapter 1: as solid birch trees that bend in the winter storms, but remain resilient, or as a profession suffering from osteoporosis – decisive forces are how working conditions develop and how the profession manages its internal cleavages and distinctions.

How journalism develops as a profession also has a fundamental relevance beyond the interest of professional workers. Journalism plays a vital and acknowledged role in democracy and public debate. A central premise of the media welfare state is that journalism is a collective and public good. The aim of media policy is to secure diversity and an independent journalism that serves society in a good way. Consequently, society is obliged to pay attention to journalists' working conditions because they are connected to the kind of journalistic content the professionals are able to produce. Union density is high in Norway, and the Nordic model values collective agreements and equality in working life. As Cohen and de Peuter (2020) state, if journalism is to have a future, it must be organized. Unionization in journalism represents continuity through change rather than disruption and novelty (Cohen and de Peuter, 2020, p. xii). Collective solutions within the Nordic model are a vital key to securing a resilient journalism in the future and thus to fortifying journalism as a democratic infrastructure in society. The same goes for public support and subsidies within the context of the media welfare state. Journalism constitutes an adaptable and changeable profession, containing a diverse range of professionals carrying out their work in a variety of forms. Even if the profession experiences disruption and the internal landscape slides, a professional core will remain. Here, the professional collective and societal acknowledgment constitute essential keys in future development.

This book has discussed some of the tensions and challenges that journalism faces as a profession. A limitation is that the empirical chapters have focused on only some parts of the profession, such as freelancers, newcomers, and columnists. The book does not entail any study of typical news journalists in traditional newsrooms, for example, who relate to metrics in their daily tasks, work rotational shifts, and experience heavy time pressures. Here, also the relation between specialized beat reporting and generalists is of interest. To fully understand how journalistic work develops, as well as how it is perceived and understood among the professionals carrying it out, a newsroom study would add relevant information to existing knowledge. For further research into the field of journalism, such extensive newsroom studies, including observation as a method, could contribute vital understanding.

References

Beck, U. (2000) *The Brave New World of Work.* Cambridge: Polity Press.

Broersma, M. (2013) A refractured paradigm: Journalism, hoaxes and challenge of trust. In Peters, C. & Broersma, M. (eds). *Rethinking Journalism. Trust and Participation in a Transformed News Landscape.* London: Routledge, pp 28–45.

Carlson, M. (2015) Introduction: The many boundaries of journalism. In Carlson, M. and Lewis, S. (eds.) *Boundaries of Journalism. Professionalism, Practices and Participation.* London and New York: Routledge, pp. 1–19.

Cohen, N.S. (2016) *Writers' Rights: Freelance Journalism in a Digital Age.* Montreal & Kingston: McGill-Queen's University Press.

Cohen, N.S., Hunter, A. and O'Donnell, P. (2019) Bearing the burden of corporate restructuring: Job loss and precarious employment in Canadian journalism. *Journalism Practice*, 13(7), pp. 817–833. DOI: 10.1080/17512786.2019.1571937

Cohen, N. S and de Peuter, G. (2020) *New Media Unions. Organizing Digital Journalists*. London: Routledge.

Cook, T.E. (1998) *Governing with the News: The News Media as a Political Institution*. Chicago: University of Chicago Press.

Deuze, M.(2008) What is journalism? Professional identity and ideology of journalists reconsidered. *Journalism*, 6(4), pp. 442–464. London. Sage Publications. DOI: 10.1177/1464884905056815

Gollmitzer, M. (2014) Precariously employed watchdogs? *Journalism Practice*, 8(6), pp. 826–841. DOI: 10.1080/17512786.2014.882061

Guo, L. and Volz, Y. (n.d.) (Re)defining journalistic expertise in the digital transformation: A content analysis of job announcements. *Journalism Practice*, 13(10), pp. 1294–1315. DOI: 10.1080/17512786.2019.1588147

Hess, K. & Waller, L. 2017. *Local Journalism in a Digital World*. London: Palgrave.

Hovden, J.F. (2008) *Profane and sacred: a study of the Norwegian journalistic field*. Phd-thesis, University of Bergen.

Hvid, H. and Falkum E. (eds.) (2019) *Work and Wellbeing in the Nordic Countries. Critical Perspectives on the World's Best Working Lives*. London and New York: Routledge.

Iversen, B. (2020) Nye nettpublikasjoner, nye informasjonsstrømmer. [New digital publications and new streems of information]. In Ravnå, P.B, Mathisen, B.R. and Jorgensen, S.H (eds.) *Meningsdanning, deltakelse og kommunikasjon i demokratiske samfunn*, Stamsund: Orkana Akademisk. pp. 195–218.

Kalleberg, A.L. (2018) *Precarious Lives. Job Insecurity and Well-being in Rich Democracies*. Cambridgde: Polity Press.

Kalleberg, A.L. and Vallas, S.P. (eds) (2018) *Precarious Work: Causes, Characteristics, and Consequences. Research in the Sociology of Organizations*. Vol. 31. Bingley, UK: Emerald.

Küng, L. (2015) *Innovators in Digital News*. London: I.B Taurus.

Lamark, H. and Morlandstø, L. (2019) Snakker journalister fortsatt med folk? In Bjerke, P., Fonn, B.K. and Mathisen, B.R. (eds.) *Journalistikk, profesjon og endring*. Stamsund: Orkana Akademisk. [Journalism, a profession in change].

Le Masurier, M. (2015) What is slow journalism? *Journalism Practice*, 9(2), pp. 138–152. DOI: 10.1080/17512786.2014.916471

Mathisen, B.R. (2013) *Gladsaker og suksesshistorier. En sosiologisk analyse av lokal næringslivsjournalistikk i spenning mellom lokalpatriotisme og granskningsoppdrag. [Positive stories about success. A sociological analysis of local journalism in the tension between local patriotism and critical watchdog ideal]*. PhD dissertation. Bodø: Universitetet i Nordland.

Mathisen, B.R. (2016) Entrepreneurs and idealists: Freelance journalists at the intersection of autonomy and constraints. *Journalism Practice*, 11(7), pp. 909–924. DOI: 10.1080/17512786.2016.1199284.

Mathisen, B.R. & Morlandstø, L. (eds.) (2019) *Blindsoner og mangfold: en studie av lokaljournalistikken i lokale og regional medier*. Stamsund: Orkana Akademisk [Blind spots and diversity – a study of local journalism].

Morlandstø, L. and Mathisen B.R. (2016) Participation and control. The interaction between editorial staff, technology and users in online commentary journalism. *Digital Journalism*, 5(6), pp. 791–808. DOI: 10.1080/21670811.2016.

Naldi, L. and Picard, R.B. (2012) Let's start an online news site: Opportunities, resources, strategy and formational myopia in start ups. *Journal of Media Business Studies*, 4, pp. 47–59.

Norbäck, M. (2021) Back to the future of journalist work? Entrepreneurial subjectivity and freelance journalism in Sweden. *Journalism*, pp 1–18. DOI:10.1177/14648849211033131

Olsen, K.S. (2018) *Tradisjonsforankrede og digitaldreide lokaljournalister. En hverdagssosiologisk studie av norsk lokaljournalistikk i en brytningstid.* Phd-dissertation. Bodø: Nord University [Traditionally Anchored and Digitally Oriented Local Journalists. An Everyday Life-Sociological Study of Experiences and Tensions among Norwegian Local Journalists].

Rafter, K. (2016) Introduction. *Journalism Practice*, 10(2), pp. 140–142. DOI: 10.1080/17512786.2015.1126014

Ryfe, D. (2016) News institutions. In Witschge, T., Anderson, C.V., Domingo, D. and Hermida, A. (eds.) *The SAGE Handbook of Digital Journalism*. Los Angeles: SAGE.

Schudson, M. (2013) Would journalism please hold still!. In Peters, C. and Broersma, M. (eds.) *Rethinking Journalism. Trust and Participation in a Transformed News Landscape*. London: Routledge, pp. 191–199.

Smeaton, D. (2003) Self-employed workers: Calling the shots or hesitant independents? A consideration of trends. *Work, Employment and Society*, 17(2), pp. 379–391. London. Sage Publications.

Steensen, S. & Kalsnes, B. (2020) Fra fast lokaljournalist til midlertidig digitalt hode. *Norsk Medietidsskrift*, 27(1), pp. 1–20. [from local journalist to temporarily digital head]

Vallas S.P. and Christin A. (2018) Work and identity in an era for precarious employment: How workers respond to 'personal branding' discourse. *Work and Occupations*, 45(1), pp. 3–37. DOI: 10.1177/0730888417735662

Wagemans, A., Witschge, T. and Deuze, M. (2016) Ideology as resource in entrepreneurial journalism. *Journalism Practice*, 10(2), pp. 160–177. DOI: 10.1080/17512786.2015.1124732

Waschková Císařová, L. (2017) The voice of the locality. In Waschková Císařová, L. (ed.) *Voice of the Locality: Local Media and Local Audience*. Prague: Masaryk University, pp. 19–38.

Wiik, J. (2015) Internal boundaries: The stratification of the journalistic collective. In Carlson, M. and Lewis, S. (eds) *Boundaries of Journalism. Professionalism, Practices and Participation*. London and New York: Routledge, pp. 118–133.

Witschge, T. and Nygren, N. (2009) Journalism: A profession under pressure? *Journal of Media Business Studies*, 6(1), pp. 37–59. DOI: 10.1080/16522354.2009.11073478

Zelizer, B. (2004) *Taking Journalism Seriously: News and the Academy*. London: Sage.

Index

120   *Index*

Printed in the United States
by Baker & Taylor Publisher Services